Thank you for choosing our recipe book. At FoxFit we understand that the most important part of achieving any fitness goal is nutrition.

We believe in helping people achieve their goals through a sustainable and enjoyable plan. We do not believe in super strict diets or cutting out food groups. Instead, we would like to teach you how to understand nutrition, break down any unhealthy relationships you have towards food and enjoy tasty meals whilst you work towards your health and fitness goals.

Using the recipes in this book along side a FoxFit fitness and nutrition plan is a great way to help you improve your nutrition, boost your energy and leave you looking and feeling fantastic.

Visit our website to discover more on how we can help you to accelerate towards your fitness goal and achieve the head turning, compliment gaining results you have always wanted.

WWW.FOXFITPT.COM

I hope you enjoy all the mouth watering recipes that are waiting for you inside.

Russell Fox

BREAKFAST

BACON 'N' EGGS

PACKED LUNCHES

INGREDIENTS

6 Eggs

2 rashers Bacon

1 small Onion, finely diced

1 tsp dried Oregano

½ tsp of Chilli Powder

1 tbsp Olive Oil

METHOD

1. Preheat oven to 180c (160f), 350f, Gas Mark 4. Line a muffin tin with 4 paper cases.

2. In a bowl whisk the eggs & seasoning together.

3. In a small frying pan, using the olive oil, fry the bacon until crispy. Allow to cool slightly. And chop/crumble the bacon.

4. Add the bacon & onion to the egg mix. Beat well & divide between the 4 muffin cases. Bake in the oven for 10-15 minutes until firm.

5. These savoury muffins can be eaten chilled & taken to work in lunchboxes.

MY NOTES

124KCAL 13.2G FAT 10.2G PROTEIN 3.2G CARBS SERVES4

HERBY SAUSAGES

INGREDIENTS

225g Pork Mince

2 tsp Salt

2 tsp Ground Peppercorns

2 tsp fresh Sage, finely chopped

2 tsp fresh Basil, finely chopped

2 tbsp Coconut Oil

METHOD

1. In a large bowl mix together the pork mince with the salt, pepper, sage and paprika. Combine well. Cover & chill in fridge overnight.

2. Make the meat mixture into 12 sausage shapes.

3. Melt coconut oil in large non-stick frying pan. Over a medium heat cook the sausages until well brown & thoroughly cooked through. Allow 4 sausages per person.

MY NOTES

260 KCAL | 23G FAT | 13.3G PROTEIN | 0G CARBS | SERVES 3

BANANA NUT SHAKE

MEAL FOR ONE

INGREDIENTS

1 Banana

200ml Almond Milk

2 tbsp Natural Yogurt

2 tsp Brewer's Yeast Powder

3-4 ice cubes

METHOD

Place all the ingredients in a high power blender & blend until smooth. Serve immediately.

MY NOTES

199KCAL | 3G FAT | 7G PROTEIN | 26G CARBS | SERVES 1

BREAKFAST STEAK

MEAL FOR ONE

INGREDIENTS

125g thin Rump Steak

150g Tomatoes

1 tbsp Olive Oil

3 tbsp fresh Basil, chopped

1 tbsp fresh Parsley, chopped

Salt & Pepper to own taste.

METHOD

1. Skin & chop the tomatoes.

2. In a frying pan, heat the oil and add the steak. Quickly fry for 2-3 mins until browned on both sides. remove & place to one side. Allow to rest.

3. Next add the chopped tomatoes and cook for 3-5 mins. Add seasoning & herbs. Serve immediately with the steak.

MY NOTES

464 KCAL | 32G FAT | 38G PROTEIN | 6G CARBS | SERVES 1

SALMON WRAPS

INGREDIENTS

1 packet of Asparagus Spears

125g Smoked Salmon

1 Lemon, quartered

5 grinds of Black Peppercorns

METHOD

1. Lightly steam asparagus spears for 2-3 mins so they still have crunch/bite.

2. Wrap bundles of spears with smoked salmon slices. Squeeze over lemon juice & sprinkle with black pepper.

MY NOTES

261KCAL 13G FAT 31G PROTEIN 5G CARBS SERVES 2

AVOCADO & GRAPEFRUIT SALAD

MEAL FOR TWO

INGREDIENTS

2 Grapefruits

2 Oranges

2 Avocados

1 tbsp fresh Mint, chopped

METHOD

1. Peel both the oranges & grapefruits. Remove all the pith. Cut the fruits into segments. Remove the flesh from the avocados & slice.

2. Arrange all the ingredients on the plates, sprinkle with mint & serve.

MY NOTES

242.3 KCAL | 13.5G FAT | 3.2G PROTEIN | 27G CARBS | SERVES 2

ENGLISH FRITTATA

INGREDIENTS

4 Debbie & Andrew Sausages, sliced

4 rashers Bacon, chopped

150g Button Mushrooms, halved

8 large Eggs Whites

3 tbsp Almond Milk

140g Cherry Tomatoes, halved

400g tins Cannellini Beans, drained & rinsed

2 tsp Smoked Paprika

small bunch of Chives, sniped

3 tbsp Tomato Puree

1 tbsp Worcestershire Sauce

METHOD

1. Preheat oven to 180c (160 fan), 350f, Gas Mark 4. Using a little olive oil grease & line base of a baking tin.

2. In a large frying pan, cook bacon & sausages until browned all over. Stir often to stop them from sticking to pan. Place them in baking tin.

3. Next fry mushrooms for about 5mins until golden. Add these to the tin too.

4. In a bowl whisk egg whites with milk & pour into tin. Top with tomatoes. Bake in oven for 20-25 mins.

5. Meanwhile in a saucepan, tip in beans, a little water, tomato puree & Worchester sauce. Stir & heat through.

6. Scatter chives on frittata. Cut into wedges & serve beans on the side.

MY NOTES

343.8 KCAL | 17G FAT | 28G PROTEIN | 19.7G CARBS | SERVES 4

AVOCADO &SALMON

INGREDIENTS

2 ripe Avocado

200g tin Salmon, drained & flaked

3 tbsp Quark

1 small Onion, finely diced

1 tsp Smoked Paprika

3 tbsp Lemon Juice

METHOD

1. Stone the avocados. Carefully remove the flesh & dice.Toss in lemon juice.

2. In a bowl mix together the quark, onion, salmon & paprika. Add the avocado & mix again. Serve either in the avocado skins or in a small bowl.

MY NOTES

443.5 KCAL | 29.5G FAT | 25G PROTEIN | 19.5G CARBS | SERVES 2

BERRY CRUMBLE

MEAL FOR TWO

INGREDIENTS

50g unsweetened Desiccated Coconut

100g Almond Flour

50g chilled Butter, cubed

250g frozen Mixed Berries

4 tbsp Coconut Cream

1 tsp Vanilla Extract

METHOD

1. In a small saucepan bring berries & vanilla extract to a simmer for 5 mins.

2. In a bowl mix the dessicated coconut with the almond flour & rub in the butter to form a crumbly mix.

3. Place the berries in an ovenproof dish & top with the almond mix.

4. Grill for 5 mins, careful not to burn the top. Serve with 1tbsp coconut cream per person.

MY NOTES

339.6 KCAL | 28G FAT | 6.7G PROTEIN | 15.2G CARBS | SERVES 2

HASH BROWNS & BACON

INGREDIENTS

3 medium Sweet Potatoes

2 tbsp Olive Oil

½ tsp dried Chives

½ tsp dried Parsley

½ tsp Chilli Powder

12 rashers Bacon

2 tbsp Maple Syrup

Salt & Pepper to own taste

METHOD

1. Peel & grated sweet potatoes into a large bowl. Toss through herbs, spices & seasoning.

2. In a non-stick pan heat the oil over a medium heat,add the grated potato & stir occasionally until cook through. Takes about 10 mins.

3. Meanwhile place bacon under a hot grill, drizzle the rashers with a little maple syrup. After 3-4 mins turn the bacon, drizzle again & cook for a further 3-4 mins.

MY NOTES

301 KCAL | 19G FAT | 11G PROTEIN | 23G CARBS | SERVES 4

BREAKFAST BISCUITS

INGREDIENTS

150g Almond Flour

2 tsp Coconut Oil

5 whole Eggs

1 tsp Maple Syrup

METHOD

1. In a large bowl beat together all the ingredients, except the coconut oil, until it forms a dough.

2. Divide the dough into 6. Roll each piece into a ball, then flatten slightly.

3. In a non-stick frying pan, melt the coconut oil over a medium to low heat. Cook biscuits for 2 mins on each side.

MY NOTES

118 KCAL | 7.2G FAT | 5.1G PROTEIN | 9G CARBS | SERVES 6

SALMON & EGGS

MEAL FOR ONE

INGREDIENTS

100g of fresh Salmon, shredded

1 large whole Eggs

2 large Egg Whites

small Red Pepper, deseeded & diced

1 Courgette, grated

25g Butter

Salt & Pepper to own taste

METHOD

1. In large bowl whisk whole eggs, egg whites & season together. Stir in salmon, pepper & courgettes.

2. In a large non-stick frying pan over low heat gently melt butter. Tip in egg mix, stir constantly until lightly scrambled. Serve immediately.

MY NOTES

437 KCAL | 29G FAT | 35G PROTEIN | 9G CARBS | SERVES 1

MUSHROOM FRICASSEE

INGREDIENTS

250g Lardons

250g Porcini Mushrooms, quartered

250g Chanterelle Mushrooms, quartered

250g Button Mushrooms, halved

3 Shallots, finely chopped

2 Garlic cloves, finely chopped

1 small bunch Parsley, chopped

2 tbsp Walnut Oil

METHOD

1. Heat oil in large non-stick saucepan. Add lardons and fry for 2-3 mins.

2. Add garlic & shallots & saute for 1-2 mins.

3. Next add all the mushrooms & saute until soft & golden. Sprinkle over parsley, mix it in & serve immediately.

MY NOTES

252 KCAL | 20G FAT | 15.2G PROTEIN | 7G CARBS | SERVES 4

BANANA YOGURT POTS

MEAL FOR TWO

INGREDIENTS

300g 0% Total Greek Yogurt

2 Bananas, sliced

2 scoops of Banana Protein Powder

20g Walnuts, toasted

METHOD

1. To toast walnuts, heat a non-stick frying pan over a medium heat. Add the walnuts & stir until can smell the nutty aroma & are beginning to brown. Remove from heat & set to one side.

2. In a large bowl beat the protein powder into the Greek yogurt.

3. Layer banana & yogurt. Top with toasted walnuts.

MY NOTES

394KCAL	8G FAT	47.5G PROTEIN	33G CARBS	SERVES 2

GREEN TEA SMOOTHIE

MEAL FOR ONE

INGREDIENTS

240ml brewed Green Tea

1 tbsp ground Flax-seed

1 tbsp Almond Butter

1 Peach, chopped

3-4 Ice Cubes

METHOD

Puree all the ingredients in a high power blender until smooth about 2-3 mins. Serve immediately

MY NOTES

222 KCAL | 14G FAT | 7G PROTEIN | 7G CARBS | SERVES 1

CHOCOLATE PROTEIN PANCAKES

INGREDIENTS

2 whole Eggs

2 Egg Whites

1 tbsp of Almond Butter

50g Almond Flour

10g 85% Dark Chocolate

1 tbsp Coconut Oil

2 scoop Chocolate Protein Powder

4 tbsp Honey

METHOD

1. Mix egg, almond flour, whey, almond butter together in a bowl.

2. In large non-stick frying pan melt coconut oil. When oil hot pour in pancake mix. Cook for 2 mins.

3. Finish cooking under a heated grill 2-3 mins.

4. Grate dark chocolate (85%) over the pancake. Cut into 4 pieces. Serve drizzled with honey.

MY NOTES

374KCAL | 21G FAT | 22G PROTEIN | 23G CARBS | SERVES 4

BLUEBERRY YOGURT BURST

MEAL FOR ONE

INGREDIENTS

100g Greek Yoghurt

50g Blueberries

1 scoop Vanilla Protein Powder

METHOD

1. Mix 1 scoop of vanilla whey into a generous serving of full-fat Greek yogurt.

2. Swirl in a handful of frozen blueberries, top with some plain Greek yogurt & some more blueberries.

MY NOTES

296 KCAL | 12G FAT | 32G PROTEIN | 15G CARBS | SERVES 1

BANANA BREAD MUFFINS

INGREDIENTS

300g Almond Flour

6 Ripe Bananas, mashed

6 Eggs

70g Ground Flaxseed

50g Almonds, chopped

1 tsp Ginger

1 tsp Cinnamon

1tsp Baking Powder

1tsp Bicarbonate of Soda

1tsp Vanilla Extract

4tbsp Honey

METHOD

1. Preheat oven to 180c (160 fan), 350F, Gas Mark 4. Use muffin baking tray & line with paper cases.

2. In a large bowl, mix the honey, eggs, vanilla & mashed bananas. Beat well. Add almonds. In another bowl combine the flour, baking powder, bicarbonate of soda, & spices. Then gradually add the dry mix to the wet one. Beat well so doesn't become clumpy.

3. Make a well in the centre of the dry ingredients & pour the wet ingredients in. Fold the two together. Combining well.

MY NOTES

328 KCAL | 20G FAT | 12G PROTEIN | 25G CARBS | SERVES 12

FRIED SARDINES

MEAL FOR TWO

INGREDIENTS

500g fresh Sardines, scaled, gutted & cleaned

75ml White Wine Vinegar

2 Shallots, sliced

2 Garlic cloves, crushed

1 Lemon, grated rind & juice only

pinch of dried Chilli Flakes

2 tbsp Olive Oil

METHOD

1. In a saucepan, simmer the garlic, lemon juice & zest, chilli, white wine vinegar & shallots until it has reduced by half.

2. Meanwhile heat olive oil in a large non-stick frying pan and fry the sardines for 2 minutes on each side. Serve immediately with sauce spooned over the sardines.

MY NOTES

367 KCAL | 21G FAT | 45G PROTEIN | 1G CARBS | SERVES 2

CHORIZO EGGS

INGREDIENTS

150g Chorizo Sausage, diced

8 Eggs

2 Garlic Cloves, minced

small bunch of fresh Coriander, chopped

2 Red Chillies, finely chopped

1 Avocado, mashed

1 tbsp Coconut Oil

1 tbsp Smoked Paprika

METHOD

1. In a non-stick frying pan, over a medium heat, melt the coconut oil & add the onion. Fry until translucent & soft. Add chorizo & fry until it has browned & onion has caramelised.

2. In a large bowl whisk the eggs. Mix in the chillies, coriander, garlic & smoked paprika. Pour eggs into pan. And add the mashed avocado. Cook & mix, so looks like scrambled eggs. Serve immediately.

MY NOTES

359 KCAL | 30.2G FAT | 20.7G PROTEIN | 1.2G CARBS | SERVES 4

BANANA BREAKFAST PUDDING

MEAL FOR ONE

INGREDIENTS

30g Chia Seeds

50ml Coconut Milk

1 ripe Banana, mashed

1 tbsp Honey

1 tsp Vanilla Extract

1 tbsp Lemon Juice

pinch of Cinnamon

METHOD

1. Soak chia seeds in coconut milk. Mix well & allow to rest for 15 mins. Break up any lumps with a fork, stir & allow to for another 10mins.

2. Stir in all the remaining ingredients & mix well. Pour into fridge & allow to chill overnight.

3. Have for breakfast the next day. Can also be a des-sert after an evening meal.

MY NOTES

350KCAL | 10G FAT | 6G PROTEIN | 59G CARBS | SERVES 1

BASIC BREAKFAST CEREAL

INGREDIENTS

90g Coconut Flakes

50g Sunflower Seeds

100g Blanched Almonds

100g Cashews

100g Pine Nuts

100g chopped Walnuts

METHOD

1. In a non-stick large frying pan gently toast all the ingredients. Takes 10 mins.

2. Once cool, store in an airtight jar.

MY NOTES

276 KCAL | 24G FAT | 7G PROTEIN | 8G CARBS | SERVES 12

BERRY SMOOTHIE

MEAL FOR ONE

INGREDIENTS

small handful of Spinach

small handful of chopped Kale

50g Blueberries

25g Almonds

½ Banana

100ml Coconut Milk

½ tbsp Ground Flaxseed

3-4 Ice Cubes

METHOD

In a high power blender, blend all the ingredients together & serve in tall glass immediately.

MY NOTES

302KCAL | 18G FAT | 10G PROTEIN | 25G CARBS | SERVES 1

MILAN FRITTATA

INGREDIENTS

2 tbsp Olive Oil

1 Onion, thinly sliced

500g Plum Tomatoes, deseeded & diced

45g Gruyere Cheese, grated

bunch Oregano, torn

6 whole Eggs

3 Egg Whites

30g Butter

METHOD

1. Heat oil in large frying pan & saute onion until soft. Next stir in the tomatoes and cook for 1-2 mins.

2. In a large bowl whisk eggs and egg whites together until slightly frothy. Add the tomato & onion mix. Sprinkle over cheese & oregano. And stir.

3. Wipe the frying pan with kitchen towel. Add the butter and melt over a low heat. When foamy add the egg mixture. Cover with a lid or tin foil & cook on a very low heat for 30 mins.

4. Carefully run a knife around the frittata edge to loosen. Invert pan onto a plate. Cut into wedges to serve.

MY NOTES

346 KCAL | 26G FAT | 19G PROTEIN | 9G CARBS | SERVES 4

BREAKFAST EXPRESS

MEAL FOR ONE

INGREDIENTS

1 large whole Egg

3 large Egg Whites

2 handful Stir-fry Vegetable Mix

1 tbsp Coconut Oil

Salt & Pepper to own taste

METHOD

1. Heat coconut oil in large non-stick frying pan over medium heat.

2. In a bowl whisk eggs together & season.

3. Add stir-fry veg to the frying pan & pour in the eggs. Cook for 2-3 minutes. Finish omelette under hot grill for 2-3 mins.

MY NOTES

269KCAL | 21G FAT | 18G PROTEIN | 2G CARBS | SERVES 1

BREAKFAST MEATZA

INGREDIENTS

250g Pork Mince

5 Eggs

25g Almond Flour

1 heaped tsp Vine Ripened Tomato Paste

2 pre-cooked Debbie & Andrews Sausages, sliced

2 rashers Bacon, chopped

handful of Cherry Tomatoes, halved

2-3 Mushrooms, sliced

25g Cheddar Cheese in thin slices, use vegetable peeler

fresh Basil leaves

1 tsp dried Oregano

METHOD

1. Preheat oven to 160c fan, 180c fan, gas mark 4, 350f.

2. In a bowl mix 1 egg, pork mince, almond flour & oregano. Press the mix into a pizza tin. And cook for 10 minutes.

3. Brush tomato paste over the base. Add the chopped bacon & mushrooms. Put back into the oven for 10 mins.

4. Next add the tomatoes & cook for a further 5 mins.

5. Last ingredients are 4 whole eggs, the chopped sausage & the thin cheese pieces. Return to the oven for 5-7 mins.

6. Add some fresh basil leaves & serve the Meatza.

MY NOTES

399 KCAL | 30G FAT | 28G PROTEIN | 4G CARBS | SERVES 4

FEEL-GOOD SMOOTHIE

MEAL FOR ONE

INGREDIENTS

1 Kiwi, peeled

1 Avocado, flesh only

1 tbsp Pumpkin Seeds

25g Spinach

200ml Almond Milk

2-3 Ice Cubes

METHOD

Place all the ingredients in high powered blender and blend until smooth. Serve immediately.

MY NOTES

361KCAL | 33G FAT | 8G PROTEIN | 33G CARBS | SERVES 1

BREAKFAST SMOOTHIE

MEAL FOR ONE

INGREDIENTS

100ml Coconut Water

1 shot Espresso

2 handfuls of Spinach

½ Lemon

½ Avocado

1 tsp Flax Seeds

1 scoop Protein Powder

2-3 ice cubes

METHOD

1. Place all the ingredients into high powered blender & blend until smooth. Serve immediately.

MY NOTES

337KCAL | 17G FAT | 21G PROTEIN | 30G CARBS | SERVES 1

PROTEIN GUAVA SMOOTHIE

MEAL FOR ONE

INGREDIENTS

1 Guava

100ml Water

2 tbsp Honey

8 whole Almonds

1 scoop Vanilla Protein Powder

few Ice Cubes

METHOD

Peel & deseed the guava. Place all the ingredients in a powerful blender. Blend on high until smooth. Serve immediately.

MY NOTES

339KCAL | 7G FAT | 28G PROTEIN | 41G CARBS | SERVES 1

FRUITY BREAKFAST

MEAL FOR TWO

INGREDIENTS

25g Almonds

25g Mixed Dried Fruits

200g Strawberries, chopped

100g 0% Greek Yogurt

2 scoops Vanilla Protein Powder

METHOD

1. In a small bowl thoroughly mix together the whey & natural yogurt.

2. In two glasses, layer the dried fruits, strawberries, nuts & yogurt.

MY NOTES

339 KCAL | 19G FAT | 26G PROTEIN | 18G CARBS | SERVES 2

LUNCH

BORTSCH

MEAL FOR TWO

INGREDIENTS

700g fresh Beetroot, grated

1 large Carrot, grated

1 tbsp Olive Oil

1 Onion, finely chopped

1 Celery Stick, finely chopped

2 large Tomatoes, deseeded, skinned & chopped

2 Garlic Cloves, crushed

1.2 litres Vegetable Stock

1 Bay Leaf

1 tbsp Lemon Juice

METHOD

1. In a large pan heat oil & add the beetroot, carrot, celery, onion & cook over medium heat for 15 mins.

2. Add tomatoes & garlic & cook for 10 mins. Pour in stock & bay leaf. Bring to boil, cover & reduce to simmer for 1 hour.

3. Remove bay leaf, stir in lemon juice & serve.

4. If you prefer smooth soup, liquidise & then serve.

MY NOTES

325 KCAL | 10G FAT | 7G PROTEIN | 51G CARBS | SERVES 2

APPLE SCOTCH EGGS

PACKED LUNCHES

INGREDIENTS

4 Eggs, hard boiled

500g Pork Mince

1 Apple, peeled & grated

1 tbsp dried Sage

1 tbsp Mediterranean dried herbs

METHOD

1. In a mixing bowl, thoroughly mix all the ingredients except the eggs. Divide the mixture into four equal size portions.

2. On workshop lay out large piece of greaseproof paper. Using hands flatten out the mince portion. Place egg in the middle & using the greaseproof paper roll mince around the egg. Shape into a ball using hands.

3. Repeat until you have made 4 large scotch eggs.

4. Place on non-stick baking tray. Cook in oven on 160c fan, 180c normal, gas mark 3, 325F.

5. Bake for 30 mins. Turn after 15 mins.

6. Serve with green salad.

MY NOTES

393 KCAL | 29G FAT | 29G PROTEIN | 5G CARBS | SERVES 4

BACON SALAD

PACKED LUNCHES

MEAL FOR ONE

INGREDIENTS

1 Onion, cut into wedges

2 tbsp Olive Oil

50g frozen Peas

1 tsp Apple Cider Vinegar

1 tsp Dijon Mustard

2 rashers Bacon, chopped

2 handfuls of Mixed Salad Leaves, shredded

METHOD

1. Heat oven to 220c (200 fan), 425f, Gas Mark 7. Lightly oil baking sheet. Arrange onion wedges & drizzle with 2 tsp oil. Roast for 15 mins.

2. Cook peas in boiling water. 2 mins. Rinse in very cold water.

3. Whisk together 2 tsp olive oil, mustard & vinegar to make salad dressing.

4. Turn onion wedges. Drizzle with remaining oil if required. Place bacon pieces on baking sheet alongside the onions. Cook for further 12 mins.

5. In a bowl toss peas & bacon with dressing. Serve warm over salad leaves topped with roasted onions, or allow to chill for lunchbox.

MY NOTES

438KCAL | 37G FAT | 16G PROTEIN | 15G CARBS | SERVES 1

FISH SINIGANG

MEAL FOR TWO

INGREDIENTS

200g any White Fish

1 small Bok Choy, chopped

2 medium Tomatoes, cut into chunks

4 tbsp Tamarind Paste

2 tsp dried Chilli

750ml Water

METHOD

1. In a medium size saucepan combine the white fish, bok choy, tomatoes.

2. In a bowl or jug combine water & tamarind paste. Add to pan & stir in chilli powder.

3. Bring to the boil & cook for 5 mins. Ladle into bowls & serve immediately.

MY NOTES

224 KCAL | 2G FAT | 26G PROTEIN | 27G CARBS | SERVES 2

APPLE CHOPS

MEAL FOR TWO

INGREDIENTS

2 Pork Chops

1 tbsp Almond Butter

30g Walnuts, chopped

100ml fresh Orange Juice, unsweetened

1 medium Apple, chopped

1 tsp English Mustard

½ tbsp Olive Oil

METHOD

1. In a small bowl mix olive oil with mustard. Brush pork chops with this mix.

2. Heat large non-stick frying pan over a medium heat. Add pork chops cook for 6-8 mins; 3-4 per side until browned & cooked through. Set pork chops aside.

3. In the frying pan add all the remaining ingredients except walnuts. Bring to boil, reduce to a simmer. Stir occasionally. Thicken the sauce takes 3-4 mins.

Pour over the chops & top with sprinkle of walnuts. Serve with salad or freshly steamed green vegetables.

MY NOTES

468 KCAL | 32G FAT | 27G PROTEIN | 18G CARBS | SERVES 2

LAMB

BBQ

INGREDIENTS

4x100g Lamb Leg Steaks

Marinade

2 tbsp Olive Oil

2 Garlic cloves, finely chopped

1 tbsp Balsamic Vinegar

20g Mint, leaves only, chopped

METHOD

1. Cut a few slashes into both sides of the steaks & place in a dish.

2. In a bowl mix together the marinade ingredients & pour over the steaks. Make sure each steak is thoroughly covered in marinade.

3. Cover the dish & store in fridge for 4 hours or more.

4. Oil the bbq grill. Place lamb on the grill & cook for 4-6 minutes each side.

5. Serve lamb with fresh salad.

MY NOTES

219 KCAL | 15G FAT | 20G PROTEIN | 1G CARBS | SERVES 4

CHICKEN BREAST

INGREDIENTS

4 skinless Chicken Breasts

4 rashers Bacon

Marinade

4 tbsp Tomato Puree

1 tbsp Fish Sauce

2-3 drops of Tabasco

2 tsp Honey

2 Garlic cloves, crushed

METHOD

1. Cut a few slashes into both side of the chicken breasts & place in a dish.

2. In a bowl mix together the mariande ingredients & pour over the chicken breasts. Make sure each breast is thoroughly covered in marinade.

3. Cover the dish & store in fridge for 4 hours or more.

4. Oil the bbq grill. Place chicken on the grill & cook for 8 minutes each side.

5. During last 4 minutes of cooking time. Grill bacon for 2 mins each side.

6. Serve chicken & bacon with fresh salad.

MY NOTES

167 KCAL | 7G FAT | 36G PROTEIN | 5G CARBS | SERVES 4

MUSTARD CRUSTED COD

MEAL FOR ONE

INGREDIENTS

20g Butter

200g Cod

1 tsp Dijon Mustard

5g Mustard Seeds

can garnish with Lime wedges

METHOD

1. Melt 10g butter in a non-stick pan. Add cod & cook for 1 min each side.

2. Brush Cod Flesh with mustard.

3. Melt remaining butter in pan & cook until lightly brown. Sprinkle with mustard seeds & serve with green salad or beetroot salsa.

MY NOTES

278 KCAL | 14G FAT | 1G PROTEIN | 37G CARBS | SERVES 1

BUMPKIN RIBS

INGREDIENTS

1.75kg Pork Ribs

1 tbsp Honey

1 tbsp Chipotle Paste

¼ tsp Chilli Powder

¼ tsp Ground Cumin

½ tsp Mustard Seeds, crushed

2 tbsp Tomato Puree

1 tbsp Olive Oil

METHOD

1.Using all the sauce ingredients blend together in a bowl. Rub the sauce over the ribs.

2. Place ribs & sauce in sealable plastic food bag. Chill in fridge for a minimum of 4 hours.

3. Under a hot grill cook until brown & crispy. Flip the ribs & continue to cook for a further 5-7 mins. Ribs can also be cooked on a hot bbq. Let them stand for 5 mins before serving.

4. Can be stored cold in fridge & taken to work with a salad as a packed lunch option.

MY NOTES

533 KCAL | 28G FAT | 48G PROTEIN | 22G CARBS | SERVES 10

ARTICHOKE OMELETTE

MEAL FOR TWO

INGREDIENTS

7 large Eggs

½ jar of Artichoke Hearts, drained

25g Parmesan, grated

handful fresh Basil, shredded

2tsp dried Mixed Herbs

2 tsp Coconut Oil

Pepper to season to own taste

METHOD

1. Separate 5 eggs. In a bowl beat together 5 yolks with 2 whole eggs. In a different bowl whisk 5 egg whites until stiff & fold into egg yolk mix.

2. Fold in artichoke, dried herbs, basil & season to own taste.

3. Heat grill to high. Meanwhile heat large non-stick frying pan over high heat. Add coconut oil, when melted, pour in omelette mix. Lower heat to very low. Cook for 5 minutes.

4. Scatter parmesan over the top of the omelette & finish cooking under the grill. About 3 mins.

5. Cut into wedges & serve with fresh green salad.

MY NOTES

404 KCAL | 29G FAT | 24G PROTEIN | 11G CARBS | SERVES 2

CHINESE CHICKEN

INGREDIENTS

8 Chicken Thighs

Marinade

2 Lemons, juice only

thumb-sized piece Ginger, grated

2 Garlic cloves, crushed

1 tbsp Fish Sauce

2 tsp Chinese 5 Spice

2 tbsp White Wine Vinegar

METHOD

1. Cut a few slashes into both side of the chicken thighs & place in a dish.

2. In a bowl mix together the marinade ingredients & pour over the chicken. Make sure each thigh is thoroughly covered in marinade.

3. Cover the dish & store in fridge for 4 hours or more.

4. Oil the bbq grill. Place chicken on the grill & cook for 6-8 minutes each side.

5. Serve 2 chicken thighs per person with fresh salad.

MY NOTES

292 KCAL | 19G FAT | 19G PROTEIN | 10G CARBS | SERVES 4

AUBERGINE PATE

PACKED LUNCHES

MEAL FOR TWO

INGREDIENTS

2 large Aubergines

3 tbsp Tahini

1 tbsp Lemon Juice

1 Garlic Clove, crushed

handful of fresh Parsley, chopped

Salt & Pepper to own taste

METHOD

1. Preheat oven to 200c (180 fan) 400f, Gas Mark 6.

2. Prick the whole aubergines with small sharp knife. Place on baking tray in oven & bake for 30 mins.

3. Allow to cool. Remove stalks. Chop the flesh & place into food processor along with the other ingredients. Will need to use high powered pulse & stir ingredients as forms a thick paste.

4. Dispense into four ramekins. Cover with foil & chill in fridge.

5. Serve with vegetable crudités

MY NOTES

187 KCAL | 15G FAT | 6G PROTEIN | 9G CARBS | SERVES 2

BACON TOMATOES

INGREDIENTS

8 large Tomatoes

2 tbsp Olive Oil

1 Red Pepper, deseeded & dices

1 Courgette, diced

1 Aubergine, diced

1 Onion, peeled & diced

75g Bacon, diced

75g Ham, diced

1 Garlic clove, crushed

25g Almond Flour

30g Parmesan, grated

1 whole Egg

Salt & Pepper to own taste

bunch mixed fresh Herbs, finely chopped

METHOD

1. Cut tops off tomatoes, scoop out inner & sprinkle hollow with a little salt. Turn upside down & allow juices to drain out of tomato.

2. In a large non-stick frying pan heat 2 tbsp olive oil add the vegetables & saute for 5 mins until soft. Drain the vegetables & allow juices to drain through a sieve. Give it a few shakes to release more juice.

3. Preheat oven to 180c (160 fan), 350f, Gas Mark 4.

4. In a large bowl mix drained vegetables, parmesan, egg, bacon, ham, almond flour & herbs. Stuff tomatoes with this mix & replace tops.

MY NOTES

292KCAL | 19G FAT | 19G PROTEIN | 10G CARBS | SERVES 4

ARTICHOKE SOUP

INGREDIENTS

1 Onion finely diced

400g Artichokes, finely chopped

300ml Vegetable Stock

50ml Double Cream

2tsp crushed Garlic

2 tbsp Olive Oil

25g grated Parmesan

1 tbsp dried Oregano

Salt & Pepper to own taste

METHOD

1. Heat olive oil in large saucepan over a medium heat. Stir in onion & cook until golden. Add stock & garlic. Bring to the boil.

2. Next add artichokes & oregano. Reduce heat & simmer for 20 mins.

3. Blend with cream and parmesan until smooth. Serve immediately.

MY NOTES

354KCAL | 16G FAT | 10G PROTEIN | 44G CARBS | SERVES 2

FIG SALAD

MEAL FOR ONE

PACKED LUNCHES

INGREDIENTS

3 slices of Orange

2 fresh Figs, quartered

25g Baby Spinach

30g Parmesan Cheese, shaved

1 tsp Olive Oil

Black Pepper

METHOD

Assemble salad ingredients together. Drizzle with olive oil & season with black pepper. Serve immediately

MY NOTES

242KCAL 14G FAT 15G PROTEIN 14G CARBS SERVES 1

BACON & LENTIL SALAD

MEAL FOR ONE

PACKED LUNCHES

INGREDIENTS

200g tin Green Lentils, drained & rinsed

½ tsp crushed Garlic

1 Spring Onion, sliced

½ tbsp Balsamic Vinegar

1 tbsp fresh Herbs, chopped

2 rashers Bacon, chopped

½ tbsp Olive Oil

METHOD

1. Add oil to non-stick frying pan on medium heat. Then add onion & garlic and fry for 2 mins.

2. Next add bacon & fry for further 3 mins.

3. Stir in lentils, vinegar, herbs & cook for further 2 mins.

4. Leave to cool & store in lunchbox until required.

MY NOTES

342KCAL | 16G FAT | 24G PROTEIN | 39G CARBS | SERVES 1

MINCE PROVENCAL

INGREDIENTS

225g Beef Mince

1 Onion, chopped

2 Peppers, chopped

2 Garlic cloves, crushed

1 tbsp Olive Oil

400g tin Chopped Tomatoes

3 medium Tomatoes, sliced

1-2 tbsp Herbs de Provence

METHOD

1. Preheat oven to 180c (160 fan) 350f, gas mark 4.

2. In a large pan heat the olive oil & add the peppers, garlic, onions. Fry for 5 mins.

3. Next add the mince & 1 tbsp of herbs. Stir into the vegetable mix, breaking up clumps of mince. Do this until browned all over.

4. Add the tin tomatoes, stir & allow to simmer for 5 mins. Pour the contents into an ovenproof dish. Top with sliced tomatoes & sprinkle with remaining herbs. Bake in the oven for 20 mins. Serve with green vegetables.

MY NOTES

344 KCAL | 14G FAT | 30G PROTEIN | 29G CARBS | SERVES 2

HEAVENLY HALLOUMI SALAD

PACKED LUNCHES

INGREDIENTS

500g Halloumi

150g Radishes

150g Sugar Snap Peas

½ Cucumber, cut in batons

Dressing

1 tbsp White Wine Vinegar

1 tsp Honey

1 tsp Dijon Mustard

2 tbsp Quark

METHOD

1. Make dressing in small bowl by stirring together vinegar,honey, Dijon mustard. Toss halloumi slices in ½ of the dressing. Remove to a plate.

2. On a medium heat, place dry griddle pan. Cook for halloumi for 5 mins. Turning. Looking for a brown colour. You can also cook under a hot grill.

3. Whisk the quark into the remaining dressing. Toss through the radishes, peas & cucumber.

4. Serve the salad with the halloumi. This can be a lunchbox meal & stored in the fridge until required.

MY NOTES

302 KCAL | 17G FAT | 34G PROTEIN | 3G CARBS | SERVES 6

SALAD NICOISE

MEAL FOR TWO

INGREDIENTS

small tin of Tuna, drained

50g Green Beans, topped, tailed & steamed

1 hard-boiled Egg, quartered

8 Black Olives, halved

2 chopped Anchovy Fillets

1 tbsp Olive Oil

1 tsp Lemon Juice

1 tsp Dijon Mustard

METHOD

1. Mixed salad leaves, green beans & black olives together in a large bowl.

2. In a small screw top jar mix together the olive oil, anchovy fillets, Dijon mustard & lemon juice. Pour over salad & toss in well.

3. Top with eggs & tuna.

MY NOTES

386 KCAL | 22G FAT | 37G PROTEIN | 10G CARBS | SERVES 2

BAKED MEXICAN EGG

MEAL FOR ONE

INGREDIENTS

55g Minced Beef

½ tbsp Olive Oil

½ Garlic clove, crushed

¼ Onion, chopped.

100g tin Chopped Tomatoes

½ small Chilli, deseeded & diced

½ Courgette, grated

2 tsp Tomato Puree

¼ tsp Chilli Powder

¼ tsp Smoked Paprika

1 whole Egg

METHOD

1. Preheat oven to 180c (160 fan), 350f, Gas Mark 4.

2. In a large saucepan heat oil & add the onion and garlic. Fry for 5 mins over medium heat until soft. Add beef & cook until starting to brown.

3. Stir in tomatoes, pepper, courgettes, puree & spices. Cook for 20 mins. Spoon into a ramekin.

4. Break an egg into the ramekin. Bake in oven for 5-10 mins. Serve immediately.

MY NOTES

262KCAL 16G FAT 19G PROTEIN 7G CARBS SERVES 1

SPICY VEGGIE BURGERS

MEAL FOR TWO

HOT N SPICY

INGREDIENTS

1 small Onion, diced

zest of 1 Lemon

410g tinned Chickpeas, drained

1 large Carrot, grated

31g fresh Coriander

1 tsp Harissa

1 small Egg, beaten

1 tbsp Olive Oil

METHOD

1. Place all the ingredients, except the egg & oil, into a food processor & blitz. Slowly add egg until until mixture starts to bind. You will not need to use all the egg.

2. Form the mix into 4 burgers and chill in the fridge for 2 hours or more.

3. Brush each burger with a little oil before grilling. Grill for 5 mins each side.

MY NOTES

359 KCAL | 15G FAT | 15G PROTEIN | 43G CARBS | SERVES 2

AVOCADO & CHILLI SOUP

INGREDIENTS

2 Avocados, flesh

690ml Stock

115g Green Chillies, chopped

1 Onion, chopped

2 tbsp Lemon Juice

METHOD

1. Blend all the ingredients together until smooth & then heat through. Serve immediately.

MY NOTES

309KCAL | 24G FAT | 6G PROTEIN | 25G CARBS | SERVES 2

BEEF & CARROT NOODLE SALAD

MEAL FOR TWO

INGREDIENTS

250g Steak

1 tbsp Olive Oil

3 medium Carrots

½ Onion, thinly sliced in rings

100g Baby Spinach

Dressing

28g fresh Parsley

3 tbsp Nut Butter

1 tsp crushed Garlic

25ml Olive Oil

2 Lemon, juice only

1 Red Chilli,deseeded & chopped

METHOD

1. Rub steak with olive oil & cook on a heat griddle for 1½ mins each side rare, 2 mins medium, 3 mins well done. Rest steak for 5-10 mins.

2. In a blender blitz all the dressing ingredients.

3. Using a vegetable peeler create thin slices of carrot & then slice these into very thin strips to make carrot noodles.

4. Slice steak into strips. Then divide the baby spinach, onion, carrots & beef between two plates before dizzling with dressing.

MY NOTES

497 KCAL | 34G FAT | 32G PROTEIN | 19G CARBS | SERVES 2

CAJUN CAULIFLOWER BURGERS

INGREDIENTS

1 chopped Red Onion

1 Cauliflower grated

1 Sweet Potato

100g Almond Flour

2 Eggs

1 tsp Turmeric

1 tbsp Cajun Spice

1 tsp crushed Garlic

bunch of torn Basil

bunch of torn Parsley

METHOD

1. Cut sweet potato into 3 pieces & microwave on high for 10 minutes.

2. Peel & place flesh in food processor.

3. Add all the other ingredients & blend until there are no chunky pieces of veg.

4. Form dough into 10 burgers & place on baking sheet. Bake for 30 minutes on a medium heat.

MY NOTES

108KCAL | 7G FAT | 5G PROTEIN | 7G CARBS | SERVES 10

BALSAMIC CHICKEN SALAD

PACKED LUNCHES

MEAL FOR ONE

INGREDIENTS

150g cooked Chicken Breast, diced

½ Apple, diced

1 Spring Onion, sliced

10g Chopped Walnuts

30g Celery, chopped

2 Kos Lettuce leaves, shredded

¼ Cucumber, diced

¾ tbsp Balsamic Vinegar

1 tbsp Olive Oil

METHOD

1. In a small bowl mix together the balsamic vinegar & olive oil.

2. In a large bowl toss together all the ingredients with the salad dressing. Suitable for packed lunch.

MY NOTES

403 KCAL | 23G FAT | 32G PROTEIN | 17G CARBS | SERVES 1

COD CEVICHE

MEAL FOR TWO

INGREDIENTS

450g Cod, fillets without skin

juice of 1 Orange

juice of 6 Limes

small Red Onion, thinly sliced

30g fresh Coriander, stalks removed

1 Red Chilli, deseeded & sliced

pinch of Salt

can garnish with Lime wedges

METHOD

1. Cut fish into 1cm cubes. Put in a glass bowl & sprinkle with salt. Set aside for 20 mins. Add orange juice & 90% of the lime juice. Submerge the fish. Cover & chill in the fridge for 2 hours.

2. Mix the onion with the remaining lime juice.

3. Use slotted spoon to serve the fish into a ceramic serving bowl or into a lunch box. Drain the onion. Lightly toss the fish with onion, chillies & fresh coriander. Serve with a green salad & if desired fresh lime quarters.

MY NOTES

298 KCAL | 2G FAT | 42G PROTEIN | 28G CARBS | SERVES 2

ASIAN SALAD

MEAL FOR TWO

PACKED LUNCHES

INGREDIENTS

50g Green Cabbage, shredded
50g Red Cabbage, shredded
50g Chinese Leaves, shredded
2 Spring Onions, chopped
3 raw Brussel Sprouts, thinly sliced
1 medium Carrot, grated
25g Bean Sprouts
25g Raisins
25g Cashews, chopped
1 tbsp Sesame Seeds

Dressing
2 tbsp Olive Oil
1 tbsp Sesame Oil
1 tbsp Apple Cider Vinegar
1 tsp Tamari
1 tbsp Tahini
2 tsp Honey
1 tsp fresh Ginger, grated

METHOD

1. Place all the dressing ingredients into a small bowl & whisk together.

2. In a large bowl toss the dressing with the salad ingredients, except cashews & sesame seeds, until well coated. The salad can be chilled in the fridge and/or taken to work in a lunchbox.

3. Sprinkle with cashews & sesame seeds on serving.

MY NOTES

428 KCAL | 32G FAT | 7G PROTEIN | 30G CARBS | SERVES 2

BLACKENED CHINESE CHICKEN

MEAL FOR ONE

PACKED LUNCHES

INGREDIENTS

1 Chicken Breast, butterfly cut

1 Corn on the Cob

1 Red Pepper

1 bag of Mixed Salad Leaves

2 tsp Honey

1 tsp Olive Oil

1 tbsp Coconut Oil

1 tbsp Chinese 5 Spice

1 tsp Soy Sauce

METHOD

1. In a small bowl mix 1 tsp of honey with Chinese 5 spice & soy sauce. Brush this marinade onto a butterfly chicken breast (cut through the width).

2. Heat griddle on medium flame with 1 tbsp coconut or olive olive. Place corn on the cob onto the griddle. Turn every 3 mins. After 10 mins the cob should be blackened in places & deep gold in colour. Remove from the griddle & allow to cool.

3. Meanwhile place chicken breast on the griddle. Depending on thickness of the breast. It should cook through after 4-5 minutes on each side.

4. Dice red pepper. Remove corn kernels with a sharp knife. Chop cooked chicken into small chunks.

5. Make salad dressing by mixing the olive oil with 1 tsp of honey.

6. Dress salad leaves with the honey/oil dressing. Toss in chicken, sweetcorn & red pepper. Put into lunchbox. Store in the fridge.

MY NOTES

450 KCAL | 22G FAT | 27G PROTEIN | 36G CARBS | SERVES 1

COURGETTE HUMMUS

PACKED LUNCHES

INGREDIENTS

2 Courgettes, peeled & chopped

1 Lemon, juiced

3 Garlic Cloves, minced

50g Tahini

1 tsp Cumin

1 tsp Smoked Paprika

3 tbsp Olive Oil

Salt & Pepper to own taste

METHOD

1. Place all the ingredients into a high powered blender & blend until smooth & thick. You may need to add a little water.

2. Divide the hummus between 4 ramekins & chill in the fridge.

3. Serve with raw vegetable crudites. Suitable for packed lunches.

MY NOTES

259KCAL 25G FAT 5G PROTEIN 5G CARBS SERVES 4

SATAY CHICKEN

INGREDIENTS

6 Chicken Drumsticks, skin removed

6 Chicken Thighs, skin removed

Marinade

1 Lime, zest & juice

2 Lemongrass stalks, chopped

5cm fresh Ginger, peeled & chopped

3 Garlic cloves

2 tbsp Nut Butter

160ml Coconut Cream

1 tsp Turmeric

1 tsp Cumin

1 tbsp dried Coriander

METHOD

1. Slash cuts into flesh of drumsticks & thighs. Place in large dish.

2. In a blender add all marinade ingredients & blend until smooth.

3. Pour marinade over the chicken & rub it in. Place in fridge for at least 2 hours.

4. Heat oven to 190c (170 fan), 375f, Gas Mark 5.

5. Line baking sheet(s) with foil & roast chicken for 1 hour. Cool. Then chill in fridge ready for lunchboxes or picnics. Serve one thigh & one drumstick per person.

MY NOTES

302KCAL | 17G FAT | 34G PROTEIN | 3G CARBS | SERVES 6

DINNER

SMOKY RIBS

SLOW COOKER

BBQ

INGREDIENTS

100g Passata

16 Short Ribs

1 tsp Cinnamon

1 tsp Paprika

2 tbsp Chinese 5 Spice

1 tsp Himalayan Rock Salt

2 tbsp Honey

1 tbsp White Wine Vinegar

1 tbsp Crushed Garlic

METHOD

1. Mix all the ingredients together in a bowl. Rub over the ribs.

2. Place them on high in slow cooker for 5 hours (or low for 8 hours).

3. Drain the ribs & place over hot BBQ for 5 mins turning every 1+ min

MY NOTES

574 KCAL | 34G FAT | 62G PROTEIN | 5G CARBS | SERVES 8

50/50 MINI BURGERS

PACKED LUNCHES

MEAL FOR ONE

INGREDIENTS

75g Lamb Mince

75g Turkey Mince

2 tsp dried Oregano

METHOD

1. Preheat oven to 180c (160 fan), 350f, Gas Mark 4.

2. In a bowl thoroughly mixed together the two minces & herbs.

3. Roll into 6 balls & flatten to make burgers.

4. Place on baking tray. No need to grease as lamb mince is fatty. Cook for 10 mins each side.

5. Serve immediately with freshly steamed greens or cool for lunchbox accompanied by green salad.

MY NOTES

309KCAL | 19G FAT | 32G PROTEIN | 3G CARBS | SERVES 1

BACON HASH

INGREDIENTS

5 rashers Bacon, chopped

900ml Chicken Stock

25g Almond Flour

25g chopped Walnuts

1 tbsp Lemon Juice

750g Sweet Potatoes, peeled & cubed

2 tsp dried Basil

Salt & Pepper to own taste

6 tbsp Olive Oil

METHOD

1. In large saucepan simmer sweet potatoes in chicken stock for 10 mins until tender.

2. Drain potatoes & return to pan, off heat) & add half the olive oil, toss & place lid on pan. Set aside.

3. Fry bacon in own fat until crispy.

4. Preheat oven to 180c (160 fan), 350f, Gas Mark 4

5. In a bowl combine almond flour, basil, lemon juice, seasoning until a crumble mixture.

MY NOTES

430KCAL 24G FAT 12G PROTEIN 43G CARBS SERVES 4

BALSAMIC STEAK

MEAL FOR ONE

INGREDIENTS

140g Sirloin Steak

1 tsp Olive Oil

Marinade

1 tsp Balsamic Vinegar

1 tsp Marmite

1 tsp Mustard

1 tsp Honey

2 tsp Olive Oil

METHOD

1. In a bowl whisk together the marinade ingredients. Pour into shallow dish. Add steak. Turn to coat it. Leave covered in fridge for 1 hour or more.

2. Heat oil on a griddle. Remove steak from marinade. Shake off excess. When griddle hot, cook steak to your liking. Serve immediately.

MY NOTES

437 KCAL | 30G FAT | 46G PROTEIN | 8G CARBS | SERVES 1

BRAISED LAMB WITH ONION

INGREDIENTS

1kg Lamb Cutlets

1 tbsp Olive Oil

2 Celery Sticks, chopped

375g whole Shallots, peeled

2 springs of fresh Rosemary

2 Bay Leaves

450ml Stock

METHOD

1. To peel shallots submerge in boiling hot water for 5-10 mins. Skin should come away easily.

2. In casserole dish heat oil, add the celery & onions and fry over a low heat for 5 mins.

3. Add the lamb pieces, 1 sprig of rosemary and bay leaves. Fry on moderate heat until meat browned on both sides.

4. Stir in the stock and add just enough water to cover lamb if necessary. Cover and simmer for 30 mins until meat is tender.

5. Serve immediately with seasonal vegetables.

MY NOTES

473 KCAL | 30G FAT | 43G PROTEIN | 6G CARBS | SERVES 6

BAKED HALIBUT

INGREDIENTS

150gx4 pieces of Halibut Steak

1 Lemon, juice only

1 tbsp sliced Almonds

100ml Almond Milk

1 tbsp Almond Butter

METHOD

1. Preheat oven to 200c (180 fan) 400f, Gas Mark 6

2. Line baking tray with foil. Place Halibut on foil. Sprinkle with lemon juice. Bake for 10 mins. Turn Halibut over, sprinkle with lemon juice again. Bake for a further 6 mins.

3. Meanwhile in non-stick frying pan toast the almonds. Stir often until lightly brown. Whisk in almond milk, almond butter & remaining lemon juice. Bring to a simmer point. Cook for one minute. Place halibut on a plate & pour over a little sauce. Serve with fresh green veg.

MY NOTES

434 KCAL | 33G FAT | 30G PROTEIN | 4G CARBS | SERVES 4

BOMBAY PRAWNS

MEAL FOR TWO

HIGHER PROTEIN

INGREDIENTS

1kg Tiger Prawns, peeled & dev-eined

1 tsp Ground Cumin

1 tbsp Curry Powder

1 tbsp Tomato Puree

50ml Lime Juice

1 tbsp Ginger, grated

1 Garlic Clove, minced

1 tsp Ground Ginger

1 tsp Garlic, minced

1 Onion, in chunks

2 tbsp Olive Oil

METHOD

1. In a food processor, blend the ginger & garlic together. Next add the onion to make a paste.

2. In a large non-stick frying pan, heat oil over low heat & add the paste. Cook for 5 mins to release the flavours. Stir in the tomato puree & sauté for another minute.

3. Add the spices & continue to sauté for a further minute.

4. Add the lemon juice & bring to a simmer. Finally add the prawns & cook for 2-3 mins.

MY NOTES

472KCAL | 16G FAT | 76G PROTEIN | 7G CARBS | SERVES 2

BACON WRAP BURGER

MEAL FOR ONE

INGREDIENTS

4 thin rashers of Streaky Bacon

100g Mince Beef

2 Tomatoes, sliced

½ Onion, finely sliced

1 tbsp Olive Olive

1 tsp Mixed Herbs

METHOD

1. In a non-stick frying pan fry the onion in olive olive. When lightly brown & soft remove from heat.

2. In a small bowl mix dried herbs into mince beef & shape into a burger. Carefully wrap the burger with the bacon slices.

3. Place on baking tray & cook in oven on 180c normal, (160c fan) gas 4, 350f for 30 mins.

4. Serve with tomatoes & onions & a side salad.

MY NOTES

459KCAL | 35G FAT | 30G PROTEIN | 6G CARBS | SERVES 1

CAJUN CHICKEN QUINOA

INGREDIENTS

500g skinless & boneless Chicken Thighs

1 tbsp Cajun seasoning

100g Quinoa

600ml hot Chicken Stock

100g Mango, peeled & cut into chunks

1 tbsp Olive Oil

400g tin Chickpeas, rinsed & drained

2 Red Onions, thickly sliced

1 Pepper, thickly sliced

1 bunch Spring Onions, chopped

small bunch Coriander, finely chopped

METHOD

1. Rinse quinoa & dry fry in non-stick pan until toasted. Will take 10-15 mins and will need to stir & break it up regularly.

2. Meanwhile cut chicken thighs into bite-sized pieces & toss through cajun seasoning. Place in baking dish & cook in oven on 180c (160 fan), 350f, gas mark 4 for 20-25 mins. May need to stir occasionally.

3. Next in a large saucepan cook quinoa over a high heat in the chicken stock for 15 mins. Stir occasionally so does not stick to base of saucepan.

4. In a large non-stick frying pan stir-fry red onions, spring onions and pepper over a high heat in olive oil until soft. About five mins. You may wish to add small splashes of water if the stir-fry dries out & starts to catch.

5. Add chickpeas & mango to quinoa. Stir in, lower heat & continue to cook for 2-3 mins. Then stir in onion & pepper mix. Cook for a further 1-2 mins.

6. Finally stir in half the chopped coriander & spoon the cajun chicken quinoa into a serving dish. Sprinkle over the remaining coriander & serve immediately.

7. Adjustments for a lower fat & lower calorie dish use skinless chicken breast & cook onions & peppers. For a spicier dish use an extra tbsp of cajun spices or add some fresh chopped chillies when cooking the onions & pepper.

MY NOTES

474KCAL | 20G FAT | 31G PROTEIN | 44G CARBS | SERVES 4

CHILLI COCONUT CHICKEN

HOT N SPICY

INGREDIENTS

8 Chicken Thighs, boned

3 Shallots

2 Garlic cloves, chopped

2 stalks Lemon Grass, chopped

16 blanched Almonds, chopped

2 tsp Turmeric

2 tsp Ground Coriander

2 tsp dried Chilli Powder

5 tbsp Coconut Oil, melted

large tin Coconut Milk

METHOD

1. Preheat oven to 190c (170 fan), 190f, gas mark 5.

2. In food processor blend lemon grass, coriander, chilli, shallots, nuts, garlic & 3 tbsp coconut oil to a paste.

3. Find a frying pan that will hold the chicken thighs in one layer or cook in batches. Add coconut oil & paste & cook for 2 mins. Next add thighs & cook thighs for 5 mins.

4. Remove chicken thighs to casserole dish. Add coconut milk to pan & stir into the paste. Pour sauce over the chicken. Cover & cook in oven for 40-50 mins. Serve immediately.

MY NOTES

471KCAL | 36G FAT | 25G PROTEIN | 16G CARBS | SERVES 4

CHILLI BEEF LOAF

HOT N SPICY

INGREDIENTS

700g Minced Beef

1 tbsp Olive Oil

½ Onion, chopped

50g Almond Flour

3 tbsp Tomato Puree

2 Red Peppers, deseeded & finely chopped

2 Chillies, deseeded & finely chopped

1 tsp Hot Chilli Powder

½ tsp Paprika

Salt & Pepper to own taste

METHOD

1. Preheat oven to 180c (160 fan), 350f, Gas Mark 4.

2. In small pan saute onion in olive oil until softened about 7 mins. Allow to cool.

3. In a large bowl mix together all ingredients including onion until thoroughly blended.

4. Fill a loaf tin (1.5 litre). Place in oven & bake for 1 hour. Drain off excess fat, turn onto board. Slice to serve.

MY NOTES

360KCAL | 17G FAT | 43G PROTEIN | 9G CARBS | SERVES 4

FISH & CHIPS

INGREDIENTS

600g Sweet Potatoes, cut into chips

4 White Fish fillets

2 Eggs, separated

2 level tbsp Almond Flour

1 tbsp dried Parsley

METHOD

1. Preheat oven to 200c fan, 220c normal, gas mark 7, 425f.

2. Put sweet potato chips into a saucepan of boiling water for 5 mins. Drain & pat dry.

3. Put egg whites into a bowl & whisk until stiff, soft white peaks. Fold in the yolks.

4. Mix almond flour with dried parsley. Dip one side of the fish onto seasoned flour & then in the egg.

5. Lightly grease baking tray. Place fish coated side up on tray. Add sweet potato chips. Cook for 15-20 minutes.

MY NOTES

374 KCAL | 13G FAT | 30G PROTEIN | 36G CARBS | SERVES 4

CHIMICHURRI STEAK

HIGHER PROTEIN

MEAL FOR TWO

INGREDIENTS

2x200g Irish Sirloin Steaks

1 tbsp Olive Oil

pinch of Himalayan Rock Salt

Dressing

½ bunch of Parsley, chopped

2 tsp crushed Garlic

½ Onion, finely chopped

½ Red Pepper, finely chopped

125ml Olive Oil

2 tbsp Apple Cider Vinegar

1 tbsp dried Chilli Flakes

METHOD

1. Make Chimichurri dressing by thoroughly mixing together all the ingredients in a small bowl.

2. Heat a grill pan/griddle on medium heat. Rub steaks with oil. Season with Himalayan or rock salt. Cook on griddle.

3. Serve with the dressing.

Steak Cooking Times

Rare – 3 minutes one side & flip. Cook for 2-3 mins

Medium – 4 mins one side & flip. Cook for 3-4 mins.

Well Done – 5 mins both sides.

MY NOTES

545KCAL 33G FAT 61G PROTEIN 2G CARBS SERVES 2

CREAMY AUBERGINE CURRY

MEAL FOR TWO

INGREDIENTS

2 Aubergines, chopped into wedges

2 Onions, chopped

2 tbsp grated Ginger

small bunch of fresh Coriander, stalks & leaves separated

2 tbsp Coconut Oil

about 20 toasted Almonds

2 tbsp Curry Powder

METHOD

1. In mini food processor,whizz together coriander stalks, ginger, almonds, curry powder & splash of water to form a paste.

2. Melt oil in large non-stick frying pan over medium heat. Fry aubergines & mushrooms for 5 mins until starting to brown & soften. Remove to a plate.

3. Add curry paste into frying pan. Stir often. Add mushrooms & aubergines back to pan. Stir in yogurt & 500ml of hot water. Simmer for 10-15 mins. Serve with scatter coriander leaves to decorate.

4. Ladle into two bowls. Garnish with remaining spring onions.

MY NOTES

349KCAL 21G FAT 13G PROTEIN 27G CARBS SERVES 2

CRAB STEW

MEAL FOR ONE

INGREDIENTS

50g Tomatoes, diced

2 Garlic Cloves, minced

100ml Fish Stock

1 Orange, juiced

1 tsp Oregano

¼ tsp Cayenne Pepper

½ Lime, flesh chopped

200g Crab Meat

METHOD

1. In a large saucepan combine tomatoes, garlic, stock, orange juice, oregano, cayenne pepper & bring to a simmer over a medium heat.

2. Reduce heat to low & simmer for 5 mins until sauce thickens. Stir in lime flesh & crab meat. Cook for a further 5 mins.

MY NOTES

249 KCAL | 1G FAT | 36G PROTEIN | 21G CARBS | SERVES 1

EASY SALMON

INGREDIENTS

2 Salmon Fillets

150ml Water

½ Lemon, juice

100ml Water

1 Onion, chopped

1 Carrot, chopped

1 Parsnip, thinly sliced

1 Bay Leaf

½ tsp dried Dill

1 tbsp Olive Oil

METHOD

1. Preheat oven to 180c (160 fan), 350f, Gas Mark 4

2. In a small pan combine water, lemon juice, water, onion, carrot, parsnip, bay leaf & dill. Bring to the boil. Once boiling, reduce heat so the juice simmers for 5 mins. Set aside.

3. Place fillets skin side down in a small baking dish, pour liquid around the fillets. Cover the fish with greaseproof paper that has been lightly brushed with olive oil. Bake for about 15 mins. Remove from oven, take away paper & allow salmon to rest in the liquid for 2-3 mins.

MY NOTES

418KCAL | 18G FAT | 64G PROTEIN | 1G CARBS | SERVES 2

MURGH CHICKEN

INGREDIENTS

8 Chicken Thighs, skinned

1 large Onion, chopped

300g Fromage Frais

1 tbsp Sultanas

70g flaked Almonds, chopped

2 tbsp Coconut Oil

8 Cardamom Pods

4 Cloves

6 Garlic cloves, peeled

2cm piece Root Ginger, peeled & chopped

2cm piece Cinnamon Stick

2 Bay Leaves

2 tsp Ground Cumin

½ tsp Paprika

½ tsp Garam Masala

METHOD

1. Put ginger, garlic, 4 tbsp of almonds & 4 tbsp water into food processor & blend into a paste.

2. In non-stick frying pan, heat 1 tsp oil & brown chicken thighs all over 5-10 mins. Set aside.

3. In a large pan add remaining oil, cinnamon, caradamom, bay leaves & cloves. Next add onion. Fry for 3-4 mins before adding paste, cumin & paprika. Stir-fry for 2-3 mins, add splashes of water if necessary.

4. Next add fromage frais & mix well. Add chicken, cover & cook over low heat for 20 mins.

5. Meanwhile toast almond flakes under a grill or fry in a non-stick frying pan.

6. Add sultanas & garam masala to chicken dish. Stir. Cook for a further 10 mins before serving with toasted almonds as garnish.

MY NOTES

456KCAL | 34G FAT | 27G PROTEIN | 11G CARBS | SERVES 4

EASY PORK FILLETS

INGREDIENTS

4 thin Pork Fillets

25g Onion, thinly sliced

1 Red Pepper, thinly sliced

1 Tomato, sliced

25ml Chicken Stock

METHOD

1. Preheat Oven to 180c (160 fan), 350f, Gas Mark 4

2. In a baking dish, line with tin foil. Lay out pork fillets. Top with the vegetables & a splash of stock. Bring the foil together to make a tent shape over the pork chops.

3. Bake for 20-25 mins until the pork is no longer pink. Open the packet & allow to brown, takes 2-3mins. Serve immediately.

MY NOTES

219 KCAL | 10G FAT | 27G PROTEIN | 6G CARBS | SERVES 4

MEXICAN PULLED CHICKEN

INGREDIENTS

400g tin Chopped Tomatoes

4 large Chicken Breasts, skinless

1 medium Onion, finely chopped

1 tbsp Olive Oil

3 Garlic Cloves, crushed

2 tbsp unsweetened Apple Juice

1 tsp Chipotle Paste

METHOD

1. Heat oil in large non-stick frying pan. Gently fry onion & garlic for about 5 mins.

2. Turn slow cooker onto HIGH. Add tomatoes, paste, onion, garlic, apple juice & stir. Push chicken breasts into sauce. Cover & cook for 2 hours.

3. Remove chicken breasts & shred the meat using two forks. Return to slow cooker & stir. Turn to LOW & cook for 30 mins.

4. Keep slow cooker on WARM until ready to serve with freshly steamed green vegetables.

MY NOTES

203 KCAL | 5G FAT | 35G PROTEIN | 6G CARBS | SERVES 4

DUCK CASSOULET

MEAL FOR TWO

INGREDIENTS

1 tbsp Olive Oil

½ large Onion, chopped

½ large Carrot, chopped

2 Garlic Cloves, minced

1 Duck Breast, precooked & sliced

1 Duck Leg, meat only

1 small Sweet Potato, cooked & cubed

150ml Chicken Stock

1 tbsp Herbs de Provence

METHOD

1. Heat oil in large saucepan over a medium heat. Add onion, carrot & herbs. Cook until vegetables are soft. Stir often. Takes about 5 mins. Add garlic & cook for a further minute.

2. Stir in duck meat, stock & sweet potato. Reduce heat. Cover & cook for 10 mins.

3. Uncover, raise heat & cook for a further 5 mins to reduce stock. Serve in bowls.

MY NOTES

319 KCAL | 14G FAT | 27G PROTEIN | 23G CARBS | SERVES2

PRAWN JAMBALAYA

INGREDIENTS

375g cooked Prawns, peeled

375g cooked Ham, diced

250g tin Chopped Tomatoes

1 Onion, chopped

1 Pepper, chopped

1 tsp Smoked Paprika

2 tbsp Coconut Oil

3 Celery Stalks, chopped

2 Garlic cloves, crushed

1 tsp dried Chilli Flakes

300g Cauliflower, grated

METHOD

1. Heat oil in large saucepan. Add ham & onions & fry over low heat for 1-2 mins. Next add pepper, garlic & celery & cook for a further min.

2. Drain juice from tomatoes & add them to saucepan along with paprika & chilli. Stir in prawns. Cover pan & cook for 10 mins. Check there is enough liquid, if not add splashes of water.

3. Add grated cauliflower. Stir & mix well. Allow to cook/warm through for 2 minutes. Serve immediately.

MY NOTES

320 KCAL | 15G FAT | 39G PROTEIN | 12G CARBS | SERVES 4

FISH FRIDAY

INGREDIENTS

375g Sweet Potato, peeled & cubed

145g Salmon Fillet

112g tinned Tuna, drained

2 Eggs

METHOD

1. Preheat oven to 180c (160 fan), 350f, Gas Mark 4.

2. In a small saucepan boil sweet potatoes in water until soft - takes about 10 mins. Drain.

3. Put all the ingredients into a food processor & blend until smooth.

4. Pour contents into a silicon loaf pan & bake for 20-25 mins until firm throughout. Serve immedieately with green vegetables or salad.

MY NOTES

212 KCAL | 6G FAT | 19G PROTEIN | 20G CARBS | SERVES 4

PROVENCAL SCALLOPS

MEAL FOR TWO

INGREDIENTS

750g Scallops

30g Coconut Flour

30ml Olive Oil

1 tbsp Parsley, chopped

1 tsp Garlic, minced

1 tsp Ground Peppercorns

1 Lemon

75ml White Wine

METHOD

1. In a large non-stick pan, heat 20ml of olive oil on a high heat. Add the scallops & lower the heat to medium.

2. Slightly brown one side of scallops before turning & browning the other side. Takes 3-4 mins in total. Add the remaining olive oil, garlic & parsley. Saute & toss the scallops for 2 mins.

3. Next add the white wine & cook for a further min. Serve scallops immediately with lemon wedges.

MY NOTES

626 KCAL | 30G FAT | 70G PROTEIN | 21G CARBS | SERVES 2

RED LENTIL DHAL

MEAL FOR TWO

INGREDIENTS

200g dried Red Lentils

2 Onions, chopped

2 tbsp Curry Powder

1 tsp Ground Cumin

1 tsp Smoked Paprika

1 tbsp Olive Oil

large tin Chopped Tomatoes

850ml Vegetable Stock

METHOD

1. Heat olive oil in large saucepan over a medium heat. Add onions & lightly fry for 2 mins. Stir in dry lentils & curry powder, cumin, paprika. Stir.

2. Add tomatoes & stock. Bring to the boil. Reduce to a simmer for 10-12 mins until lentils are soft. Season & serve immediately.

MY NOTES

421KCAL | 7G FAT | 25G PROTEIN | 26G CARBS | SERVES 2

FRUITY LAMB STEW

INGREDIENTS

450g cubed Lamb

1 tsp Ground Cinnamon

1 tsp Ground Coriander

1 tsp Ground Cumin

2 tsp Olive Oil

1 Red Onion, finely chopped

300ml Vegetable Stock

400g tin Chopped Tomatoes

1 Garlic clove, crushed

2 tbsp Tomato Puree

125g ready-to-eat Apricots

METHOD

1. Preheat oven to 180c (160 fan), 350f, gas mark 4.

2. In a large bowl mix spices together & toss the meat through to coat.

3. In a large non-stick frying pan add oil & spiced lamb. Cook for 4-5 mins until browned. Remove using slotted spoon to large casserole dish.

4. Into frying pan add onion, garlic, tomatoes & puree. Cook for 5 mins. Then add apricots & stock. Bring to the boil. Spoon over the lamb. Cover & cook in the oven for 1 hour. Remove the lid for last 10 mins.

5. Serve immediately with couscous or rice - macros not included.

MY NOTES

364 KCAL | 16G FAT | 25G PROTEIN | 22G CARBS | SERVES 4

WARRIOR CHICKEN

MEAL FOR TWO

INGREDIENTS

600g Chicken Thighs

60ml Water

2 tbsp Hoisin Sauce

2 tbsp Honey

2 tsp Ground Ginger

2 Garlic Cloves, minced

METHOD

1. Preheat oven on 180c (160 fan), 350f, Gas Mark 4.

2. Heat the water, honey, hoisin sauce, ginger & garlic in a large saucepan. Bring to a boil & then reduce heat so sauce simmers for 20 mins. Add the chicken thighs, bring heat up again & turn the thighs until they have a sticky glaze.

3. Place in a roasting dish & into the oven for 20 mins until cooked through.

4. Spoon over any remaining sauce from the sauce pan & serve immediately.

MY NOTES

523KCAL | 29G FAT | 47G PROTEIN | 19G CARBS | SERVES 2

ROAST ONION CHICKEN

INGREDIENTS

1.2kg - whole Chicken

6 tbsp Almond Butter

5 tbsp Olive Oil

200ml Chicken Stock

1 Bay Leaf

2 tsp dried Sage

2 tsp dried Rosemary

2 tsp dried Parsley

1 tsp Paprika

8 Shallots, peeled

30ml Balsamic Vinegar

Salt & Pepper to own taste

METHOD

1. Preheat oven to 220c (200 fan), 425f, Gas Mark 7. Grease roasting tin.

2. Combine the herbs & spices in a bowl and set aside. Season cavity of chicken with salt, pepper & 2tsp of herb mix. Place bay leaf inside & tie legs.

3. Brush chicken with olive oil and half the herb mix. Spoon shallots over & sprinkle with remaining herb mix. Bake for 1 hour 15 mins or until juices run clear from piercing the thigh. Cover the chicken with tin foil to keep warm.

4. Pour the juices from the roasting tin into a saucepan. & add stock. Heat & bring to the boil. Allow to simmer for 5 mins. Gradually whisk in the almond butter & stock. Serve over carved chicken.

MY NOTES

509 KCAL | 32G FAT | 46G PROTEIN | 10G CARBS | SERVES 6

CAULIFLOWER PIZZA CRUST

MEAL FOR ONE

INGREDIENTS

340g Cauliflower, grated

1 whole Egg, beaten

¼ tsp dried Basil

¼ tsp dried Oregano

¼ tsp Garlic Salt

METHOD

1. Preheat oven to 210c (190 fan), 420f, gas mark 7. Line a pizza tray with greaseproof paper.

2. Place grated cauliflower in microwave for 6 mins to soften.

3. In large bowl mix cauliflower with herbs. Add egg a little at a time until dough forms.

4. Flatten dough into pizza tray & brush with a little olive oil. Bake for 15-20 mins until golden. Remove from oven & allow to cool a little before adding toppings.

MY NOTES

211KCAL 12G FAT 13G PROTEIN 18G CARBS SERVES 1

SHEPHERD LENTIL PIE

INGREDIENTS

900g Sweet Potato, peeled & cut into chunks

200g Fromage Frais

2 tbsp Mixed Dried Herbs

1 Onion, chopped

2 Carrots, peeled & cubed

2 Celery stalks, finely sliced

2 tsp crushed Garlic

1 Red Pepper, deseeded & cubed

250ml Vegetable Stock

400g tin Chopped Tomatoes

400g tin Green Lentils

100g grated Vegetarian Cheese

1 tbsp Olive Oil

METHOD

1. Preheat oven to 180c normal, 160c fan, gas mark 4, 350f.

2. Boil sweet potatoes for 15 mins until tender enough to mash. Add fromage frais & mixed herbs. And mash until smooth.

3. In large frying pan onion & oil and stir fry until soft, about 4 mins. Add carrot, celery, garlic, pepper, stock, tomatoes. Bring to boil then reduce heat & simmer for 10 mins.

4. Drain lentils & wash. Add to the vegetables & cover. Simmer for 10 mins.

5. Place in large pie dish. Top with sweet potato mash & sprinkle with grated cheese. Cook for 20-25 mins.

MY NTOES

478KCAL | 14G FAT | 19G PROTEIN | 70G CARBS | SERVES 4

INDONESIAN STIR-FRY

INGREDIENTS

750g Beef Steaks, cubed

2 Garlic cloves, finely chopped

1 tsp dried Chilli Pepper

2 tsp Ground Coriander

2 tsp Ground Ginger

1 tbsp Fish Sauce

3 tbsp Balsamic Vinegar

2 tbsp Walnut Oil

METHOD

1. In a bowl mix together the garlic, chilli, coriander, ginger, fish sauce, balsamic vinegar.

2. Heat walnut oil in a wok. Add the beef & stir over a high heat for 2 mins. Add the spice mix & fry for a further minute. Serve immediately with cauliflower rice & steamed broccoli.

MY NOTES

350KCAL | 22G FAT | 40G PROTEIN | 0G CARBS | SERVES 4

SIDES

APRICOT STUFFING

INGREDIENTS

1 Onion, finely diced

1 tbsp Olive Oil

125g Ready-to-Eat Apricots

2 tbsp fresh Parsley, chopped

pinch of Cinnamon

75g Almond Flour

1 whole Egg, beaten

Salt & Pepper to own taste

METHOD

1. Fry the onion in the olive oil over a low heat until softened.

2. In a bowl mix all the ingredients together except the egg.

3. Slowly pour in the egg while mixing. Looking to bind the mixture but not make it too wet.

4. The stuffing can be made into small balls and roasted alongside a joint of meat. Or use to stuff cavity of a chicken before roasting.

MY NOTES

151 KCAL | 9G FAT | 5G PROTEIN | 14G CARBS | SERVES 6

BALSAMIC ROAST CARROTS

INGREDIENTS

8 medium Carrots, peeled & sliced along length into quarters

2 tbsp Olive Oil

2 tbsp Balsamic Vinegar

2 tsp Honey

METHOD

1. Preheat oven to 180c (160 fan) 450f, Gas Mark 4.

2. Bring to the boil a pan of salted water. Par boil carrots.

3. Drain and add to roasting dish. In a small bowl whisk together olive oil, vinegar & honey. Toss dressing through the carrots & roast for 15 minutes.

MY NOTES

62KCAL | 4G FAT | 1G PROTEIN | 7G CARBS | SERVES 8

BBQ GRIDDLED AUBERGINE

INGREDIENTS

2 Aubergines, sliced verti-cally

2 tbsp Olive Oil

250g Greek Yogurt

3 tbsp Nut Butter

1 Garlic clove, crushed

1 Lemon, juice only

2 tbsp Coriander, chopped

2 tbsp Parsley, chopped

2 tbsp Mint, chopped

METHOD

1. Brush each aubergine slice with some oil & place slices on bbq. Cook for for 2-3 mins on each side until golden brown and tender.

2. Mix the yogurt with the nut butter, garlic, lemon juice and herbs. Top the aubergines with yogurt dressing.

MY NOTES

197KCAL | 16G FAT | 7G PROTEIN | 6G CARBS | SERVES 6

BEETROOT SALSA

MEAL FOR TWO

INGREDIENTS

2 small cooked Beetroot, diced

4 Spring Onions, sliced

1 Red Chilli, deseeded & chopped

1 tbsp Olive Oil

1 tbsp Lime Juice

1 tbsp fresh Mint, chopped

METHOD

1. In a small bowl whisk together the olive oil, lime juice & mint.

2. Place all the salsa ingredients in a large bowl & toss together with dressing.

3. Chill in fridge for at least 30 mins before serving.

MY NOTES

91KCAL 7G FAT 1G PROTEIN 6G CARBS SERVES 2

BLUE CHEESE SPROUTS

INGREDIENTS

500g Brussel Sprouts

50g Butter

2 Onions, chopped

1 tbsp Olive Oil

50g Blue Cheese

80g Pancetta

METHOD

1. Steam Sprouts until tender. Half them along the length.

2. In a large frying pan gently heat the olive oil. Add onions & cook over low-medium heat until carmelised.

3. Add pancetta. Stir & fry for 2 mins. Next add the butter & chopped sprouts. Cook until everything warmed through & coated in butter. About 5 mins.

4. Serve with blue cheese crumbled over the sprouts.

MY NOTES

106 KCAL | 8G FAT | 5G PROTEIN | 5G CARBS | SERVES 8

BEETROOT DIP

INGREDIENTS

150g cooked Beetroot

150g Total 0% Greek Yogurt

1 tbsp fresh Chives, chopped

1 tsp Lemon Juice

METHOD

1. Finely chop 1 beetroot & set aside.

2. Add remaining beetroot, yogurt, chives & lemon juice to food rocessor & blend until smooth. Fold through remaining chopped beetroot.

3. Spoon dip into ramekins & chill the the fridge for a minimum of 15 mins before serving with crudites.

4. Suitable for sides at a BBQ or as a packed lunch.

MY NOTES

33KCAL 0G FAT 5G PROTEIN 4G CARBS SERVES 4

BRAISED CABBAGE

MEAL FOR TWO

INGREDIENTS

1 Red Cabbage, finely sliced

1 Lemon, juiced

1 tsp Salt

1 Cinnamon Stick

2 Bay Leaves

1 tbsp Maple Syrup

1 tsp Mixed Spice

250ml Pomegranate Juice

METHOD

1. Toss the red cabbage with the lemon juice & salt and set aside for 20 mins.

2. In a large saucepan add all the ingredients & genlty simmer covered for 30mins. Uncover & cont. to cook for a further 30 mins reducing the liquid. Serve immediately.

MY NOTES

327 KCAL | 1G FAT | 9G PROTEIN | 71G CARBS | SERVES 2

BBQ & MUSTARD CHIPS

MEAL FOR TWO

INGREDIENTS

250g White Potato, peeled & cut into small wedges

1 Egg White

1 tbsp dried BBQ Seasoning

1 tsp English Mustard

1 tbsp Olive Oil

METHOD

1. Preheat oven to 200c (180 fan), 400f, Gas Mark 6. Generously grease baking tray with the olive oil.

2. Parboil the potato wedges for 5 mins in small saucepan of boiling water. Drain & rinse in cold water.

3. Meanwhile whisk egg white and add bbq seasoning & mustard.

4. Coat potato wedges with seasoned egg white and spread across the baking tray.

5. Cook for 15 mins. Turn all the wedges & cook for a further 15 mins.

MY NOTES

167 KCAL | 7G FAT | 5G PROTEIN | 23G CARBS | SERVES 2

CHINESE COLESLAW

INGREDIENTS

1 whole Chinese Leaves Lettuce, shredded

1 Onion, peeled & finely diced

5 Radishes, thinly sliced

2 Celery Stalks, finely diced

2 Carrots, shredded

50g Almond Butter

3 tbsp Rice Vinegar

2 tbsp Ginger, grated

2 tbsp Fish Sauce

2 tbsp Sesame Seeds, toasted

METHOD

1. In large bowl toss together the lettuce, onion, radishes, celery, carrots.

2. In another smaller bowl whisk together peanut butter, rice vinegar, ginger, fish sauce & sesame seeds. Pour this over the vegetables and toss thoroughly.

3. Chill in fridge until ready to serve. Suitable for lunchboxes.

MY NOTES

172KCAL | 18G FAT | 7G PROTEIN | 18G CARBS | SERVES 4

CURRY SWEET POTATO WEDGES

INGREDIENTS

4 medium Sweet Potato

3 tbsp Coconut Oil, melted

2 tbsp Tikka Masala Spice

½ tbsp Cumin

METHOD

1. Preheat oven to 190c (170 fan), 375f, Gas Mark 5. Wash & cut sweet potatoes into wedges, Leave the skin on.

2. In a large bowl mix olive oil with the spices & tip in sweet potato wedges. Toss them thoroughly. Lay the sweet potatoes out on a large roasting pan. Sprinkle a little water over the potatoes.

3. Roast in the oven for 20-25 mins. Turn the potatoes every 5-10 mins.

MY NOTES

209KCAL | 11G FAT | 2G PROTEIN | 27G CARBS | SERVES 4

MUSTARD MASH

INGREDIENTS

400g White Potatoes, peeled & quartered

100ml Milk

75g Butter

2 tbsp Dijon Mustard

METHOD

1. In a pan bring slightly salted water to the boil & add the potato. Cook for 10-12 mins until the potato is soft enough to mash.

2. Drain the potatoes, add butter, milk & mustard & mash thoroughly.

MY NOTES

218 KCAL | 12G FAT | 4G PROTEIN | 25G CARBS | SERVES 4

MINT SMASHED PEAS

INGREDIENTS

50g Garden Peas

1 tsp Butter

1tsp dried Mint

METHOD

1. Boil peas for 3 mins in small saucepan.

2. Thoroughly drain.

3. Add butter & dried mint, stir in and then mash with fork or potato masher until smashed in appearance.

MY NOTES

117KCAL 8G FAT 3G PROTEIN 7G CARBS SERVERS 1

MUTTER PANEER

INGREDIENTS

300g frozen Peas

1 small Onion, finely chopped

1 tsp Garam Masala

1 tsp Curry Powder

½ tsp Turmeric

250g Cottage Cheese

2 tbsp fresh Coriander, chopped

1 tbsp Coconut Oil or Ghee

METHOD

1. Bring saucepan of water to the boil. Add the peas & cook for 2 mins. Drain & set aside.

2. In large non-stick frying pan heat oil (or ghee). Add spices, stir & cook for 30 seconds. Next add onion, stir & cook for 3 mins.

3. Add cottage cheese, stir & cook for 1 min. Finally add the cooked peas & coriander and cook for a further minute stirring gently. Serve immediately.

MY NOTES

144KCAL | 5G FAT | 11G PROTEIN | 15G CARBS | SERVES 4

HONEY ROAST SWEET POTATOES

INGREDIENTS

2 Red Onions, cut into wedges

750g Sweet Potatoes, peeled & cut into chunks

5 tbsp Olive Oil

1 tsp Ground Ginger

1 tsp Ground Cumin

½ Orange, juice only

1 tbsp Honey

METHOD

1. Preheat oven to 180c (160 fan) 450f, Gas Mark 4

2. Put sweet potatoes & red onion wedges in one layer in roasting tin. In a bowl whisk together the remaining ingredients & pour over the potatoes & onions.

3. Roast for 25-30 mins or until tender.

MY NOTES

192KCAL | 9G FAT | 2G PROTEIN | 26G CARBS | SERVES 8

CAULIFLOWER RICE

INGREDIENTS

1 large Cauliflower, grated

1 Onion, peeled & sliced

2 tbsp Coconut Oil

1 tbsp Spices own choice

METHOD

1. Melt oil in wok. Add spice & fry over low heat for 1-2 mins to release flavours & aromas.

2. Add onion & fry until soft about 4 mins.

3. Add grated cauliflower. Stirring constantly fry for 2-3 mins until warmed through & flavours have mixed in. Serve immediately.

MY NOTES

127KCAL | 8G FAT | 5G PROTEIN | 14G CARBS | SERVES4

CONDIMENTS

CHILLI & LIME DRESSING

INGREDIENTS

1 Chilli, deseeded & finely chopped

1 Lime, zest & juice

250ml Olive Oil

METHOD

Put all the ingredients in a sterilised glass jar and give it a good shake. Can be stored in the fridge.

MY NOTES

121KCAL 14G FAT 0G PROTEIN 0G CARBS SERVES 16

CITRUS DRESSING

INGREDIENTS

1 Lemon, zest & juice

1 Orange, zest & juice

1 tbsp White Wine Vinegar

2 tbsp Dijon Mustard

2 tbsp Olive Oil

METHOD

Place all the ingredients in a sterilised glass jar and give it a good shake. Can store in the fridge for up to 5 days.

MY NOTES

56 KCAL | 5G FAT | 1G PROTEIN | 2G CARBS | SERVES 6

CUMIN DRESSING

INGREDIENTS

2 tbsp Red Wine Vinegar

1 tbsp Ground Cumin

1 tsp Smoked Paprika

1 tsp dried Chilli Flakes

5 tbsp Walnut Oil

METHOD

Whisk all the ingredients in a bowl. Store in sterilised glass jar in fridge. Always give dressing a good shake before using.

MY NOTES

100KCAL | 11G FAT | 0G PROTEIN | 0G CARBS | SERVES 6

DILL DRESSING

INGREDIENTS

125ml Sour Cream

125ml Buttermilk

2 tsp Dijon Mustard

1 tbsp Dill, chopped

METHOD

Place all the ingredients in a high powered blender & blend until smooth. Can be stored in a sterilised jar in the fridge for 2-3 days.

MY NOTES

33KCAL | 2G FAT | 1G PROTEIN | 2G CARBS | SERVES 8

MINT & CHILLI DRESSING

INGREDIENTS

3 tbsp Balsamic Vinegar

2 tbsp Olive Oil

handful Mint, chopped

1 Red Chilli, chopped

1 Shallot, chopped

METHOD

Place all the ingredients into a high powered blender & blend until smooth. Can be stored in sterilised jar for up to 5 days in the fridge.

MY NOTES

81KCAL 7G FAT 0G PROTEIN 3G CARBS SERVES 4

ANCHOVY DRESSING

MEAL FOR TWO

INGREDIENTS

2 Anchovies

1 tbsp Red Wine Vinegar

3 tbsp Olive Oil

METHOD

Place ingredients in high powered blender & blend until smooth. Can be stored in a sterilised jar in the fridge for up to 2 days. Shake before use.

MY NOTES

187 KCAL | 21G FAT | 1G PROTEIN | 0G CARBS | SERVES 2

BALSAMIC MARINADE

MEAL FOR ONE

INGREDIENTS

1 tbsp Balsamic Vinegar

1 tsp Olive Oil

1 Rosemary Spring, chopped

METHOD

1. Whisk ingredients together in a small bowl.
2. Pour over chosen meat or fish & cover.
3. Marinate for 4 hours in the fridge.

MY NOTES

50 KCAL | 4G FAT | 0G PROTEIN | 3G CARBS | SERVES 1

BLENDER MAYONNAISE

INGREDIENTS

1 Egg

1 tbsp Cider Vinegar

300ml Olive Oil

pinch of dried Tarragon

METHOD

1. Break egg into blender add the tarragon and blend for 30 seconds.

2. Add the cider vinegar and blend again.

3. With motor running, slowly pour in the oil in a steady thin stream. The sauce should start to thicken after half the oil has been added.

4. Continue to pour the oil until it has all been combined.

5. Scrape mayonnaise into a sterile jar with lid and store in the fridge.

MY NOTES

122KCAL | 14G FAT | 0G PROTEIN | 0G CARBS | SERVES 20

BLUE CHEESE DRESSING

INGREDIENTS

2 tbsp White Wine Vinegar

75ml Double Cream

4 tbsp Creme Fraiche

½ Lemon, juice & zest

50g Blue Cheese

METHOD

Blend all the ingredients together in a high powered blender until smooth & serve immediately.

MY NOTES

180 KCAL | 18G FAT | 5G PROTEIN | 2G CARBS | SERVES 4

BUTTERMILK DRESSING

INGREDIENTS

1 Garlic clove, crushed

100ml Buttermilk

2 tbsp Mayonnaise (see recipe)

METHOD

Place all the ingredients in a blender & blend until smooth. Can be stored in a sterilised jar in the fridge for 2-3 days.

MY NOTES

36 KCAL 3G FAT 1G PROTEIN 2G CARBS SERVES 5

RANCH DRESSING

INGREDIENTS

2 tbsp Mayonnaise (see recipe)

1 tbsp White Wine Vinegar

½ Garlic clove, crushed

1 tbsp Dill

METHOD

Place all the ingredients into a high powered blender & blend until smooth. Can be stored in a sterilised jar in the fridge for up to 2 days.

MY NOTES

120KCAL 10G FAT 0G PROTEIN 7G CARBS SERVES 1

RASPBERRY VINGARIETTE

INGREDIENTS

100ml Red Wine Vinegar

1 tsp English Mustard

1 tbsp Olive Oil

50g Raspberries

METHOD

1. Place all the ingredients in high powered blender & blend until smooth.

2. Decant into a glass bottle & store. Dressing will need a shake before serving.

3. One serving is 1 tablespoon of the dressing.

MY NOTES

16 KCAL 1G FAT 0G PROTEIN 1G CARBS SERVES 11

HERAULT DRESSING

INGREDIENTS

6 tbsp Olive Oil

12 tbsp Red Wine Vinegar

2 tsp Ground Peppercorns

2 tsp dried Oregano

METHOD

Whisk all the ingredients in a bowl. Store in sterilised glass jar in fridge. Always give dressing a good shake before using.

MY NOTES

72KCAL | 8G FAT | 0G PROTEIN | 0G CARBS | SERVES 10

DILL DRESSING

INGREDIENTS

50g Watercress

6 tbsp Olive Oil

2 tbsp Cider Vinegar

METHOD

Place all the ingredients in a high powered blender & blend until smooth. Can be stored in sterilised jars in the fridge for up to one week.

MY NOTES

120KCAL | 14G FAT | 0G PROTEIN | 0G CARBS | SERVES 6

THOUSAND ISLAND DRESSING

INGREDIENTS

100g Cashews

6 Sundried Tomatoes

3 tbsp Lemon Juice

1 tsp English Mustard

1 Celery Stalk, finely diced

¼ Red Onion, finely diced

100ml Water

METHOD

1. Soak the cashews in water for 4 hours & drain. Also soak the sundried tomatoes until soft & drain.

2. In high powered blender blend all the ingredients together, except onion & celery. You may need to add more water. Once smooth transfer to a bowl & mix in celery & onion.

3. Let dressing rest overnight in a sealed jar before use. Should keep for 2-3 days.

MY NOTES

24KCAL | 2G FAT | 0G PROTEIN | 2G CARBS | SERVES 10

SMOOTHIES

BANANA SMOOTHIE

INGREDIENTS

2 Bananas

4 Celery Stalks

1 Apple

50g Spinach

½ Cucumber

250ml Water

2-3 Ice Cubes

METHOD

Chop all the ingredients. Place in a high power blender with water & ice. Blend until smooth. Serve immediately.

MY NOTES

209 KCAL | 1G FAT | 4G PROTEIN | 47G CARBS | SERVES 2

BEETROOT & PEAR SMOOTHIE

INGREDIENTS

75g Beetroot, peeled & diced

1 Pear, stalk removed

½ Lime, peeled

2cm of Ginger, peeled

100ml Water

2-3 Ice Cubes

METHOD

Place all the ingredients on high powered blender & blend until smooth. Serve immediately.

MY NOTES

133KCAL | 1G FAT | 1G PROTEIN | 32G CARBS | SERVES 2

CUCUMBER, ORANGE & MINT SMOOTHIE

INGREDIENTS

1 small Apple, roughly chopped

½ Cucumber, roughly chopped

1 Orange, flesh only

few Mint Leaves

100ml Water

2-3 Ice Cubes

METHOD

Place all the ingredients in a high powered blender & blend until smooth. Serve immediately.

MY NOTES

146 KCAL | 1G FAT | 3G PROTEIN | 38G CARBS | SERVES 1

CAN'T PERFUME SMOOTHIE

INGREDIENTS

1 small wedge Cantaloupe Melon

1 Apple

1 Lemon

50ml Water

Few Ice Cubes

METHOD

Skin cantaloupe melon & remove seeds. Roughly chop. Peel, core & chop apple. Squeeze juice of 1 lemon. Place all the ingredients in a high powered blender and blend until smooth. Serve immediately.

MY NOTES

120KCAL | 0G FAT | 1G PROTEIN | 29G CARBS | SERVES 1

CHOCOLATE MILK SHAKE

INGREDIENTS

2 tsp good quality Cocoa Powder, unsweetened

1 tsp Honey

30g Vanilla Whey

200ml Almond Milk

pinch of Cinnamon

3-4 Ice Cubes

METHOD

Place all the ingredients in a high power blender & blend until smooth. Serve immediately.

MY NOTES

208 KCAL | 4G FAT | 24G PROTEIN | 19G CARBS | SERVES 1

SNACKS

BANANA BREAD

INGREDIENTS

200g Almond Flour

50g Coconut Flour

1 tsp Baking Powder

1 tsp Cinnamon

100g Banana, mashed

4 Eggs

50g Coconut Oil, melted

50g Maple Syrup

METHOD

1. Preheat oven to 170c (150 fan), 325f, Gas Mark 3. Use a silicon bread loaf mould.

2. Sift dry ingredients into a large bowl. In another bowl thoroughly mix the wet ingredients. Add the dry mix & beat together until well combined.

3. Pour into loaf tin & cook covered with tin foil for 40 mins. Remove foil and continue to cook for 5-10 mins. Allow banana bread to cool in the mould before removing. It can be stored in an airtight container once cold.

MY NOTES

310KCAL | 23G FAT | 9G PROTEIN | 17G CARBS | SERVES 8

ANTS ON LOGS

MEAL FOR TWO

INGREDIENTS

2 Celery Sticks

4 tbsp Almond Butter

25g Raisins

METHOD

1. Trim end of each celery stick & cut them in half to make four sticks.

2. Fill with 1 tbsp of almond butter per stick & top with a few raisins.

MY NOTES

263KCAL | 19G FAT | 6G PROTEIN | 19G CARBS | SERVES 2

BANANA & RAISIN CAKE

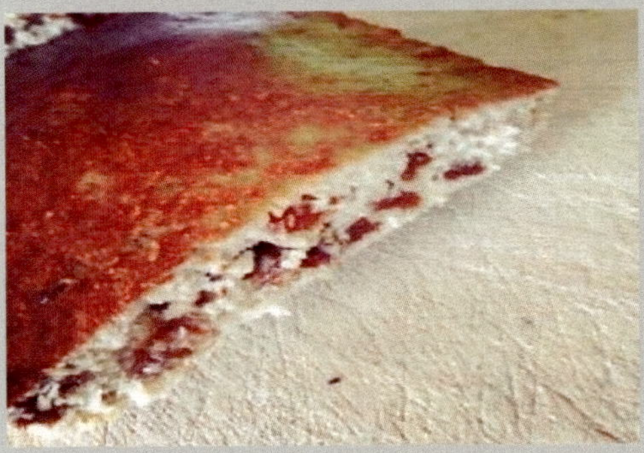

INGREDIENTS

2 ripe Bananas, mashed

50g Almond Flour

50g unsweeetened Desiccated Coconut

50g Raisins

2 whole Eggs, beaten

4 scoops Vanilla Whey

METHOD

1. Preheat oven to 180c (160 fan), 350f, Gas Mark 4.

2. In a bowl mix together all the dry ingredients & then gradually beat in the eggs until fully combined.

3. Pour into a flapjack tin & bake for 12-15 mins until cooked through. Allow to cool before cutting into squares or slices. Wrap in foil & store in airtight tin. Can also be frozen.

MY NOTES

171 KCAL | 8G FAT | 17G PROTEIN | 13G CARBS | SERVES 10

BANANA CHOCOLATE BAR

INGREDIENTS

2 Bananas

50g Almond Butter

25g Maple Syrup

2 tsp Vanilla Extract

50g Almond Flour

1 tsp Cinnamon

1 tbsp of Cocoa Powder, unsweetened

¼ tsp Bicarbonate of Soda

¼ tsp Baking Powder

1 tsp Coconut Oil

METHOD

1. Preheat oven to 170c (150 fan), 325f, Gas Mark 3. Melt coconut in rectangular baking dish in the oven. When melted brush the oil all over the dish.

2. In a food processor mix all the ingredients together & pour into the dish. Bake for 25-30 mins. Cover with foil if necessary to stop the top 'catching' i.e. burning a little.

3. Allow to cool. Cut into bars. Refrigerate. Can be taken in lunchbox to work.

MY NOTES

144KCAL | 8G FAT | 3G PROTEIN | 15G CARBS | SERVES 6

AVOCADO DIP

INGREDIENTS

225g Quark

1 Avocado

1 Garlic Clove, minced

few drops of Tabsaco

1 tbsp Lemon Juice

dash of White Wine Vinegar

METHOD

1. Mix together the quark, tabasco, garlic. Just before serving mash avocado flesh with lemon juice & white wine vinegar. Mix this into the quark to make a dip.

2. Serve with fresh vegetable crudites.

MY NOTES

219KCAL 11G FAT 18G PROTEIN 12G CARBS SERVES 2

CHOCOLATE CIRCLE

MEAL FOR ONE

INGREDIENTS

1 tbsp Coconut Oil

3 tbsp Cocoa Powder, unsweetened

50ml Maple Syrup

1 tsp Vanilla Extract

METHOD

1. In a large bowl over a pan of simmering water place cocoa chips & coconut oil. Allow to melt. Whisk in remaining ingredients.

2. Pour into silicon chocolate mould. Freeze for 30 mins.

MY NOTES

249 KCAL | 17G FAT | 3G PROTEIN | 21G CARBS | SERVES1

CINNAMON APPLE SNACKS

MEAL FOR ONE

INGREDIENTS

1 large dessert Apple

¼ tsp Cinnamon

METHOD

1. Preheat oven to 140c (120 fan), 275f, gas mark 1. Line a baking sheet with greaseproof paper.

2. Core apple & cut into very thin circular slices. Alternatively quarter the apple, remove core & seeds. Slice each quarter very thinly. Sprinkle with cinnamon on both sides of each slice to coat.

3. Spread slices out on baking tray & bake for 1 hour. Cool on wire rack to crisp the slices.

MY NOTES

110KCAL | 0G FAT | 1G PROTEIN | 29G CARBS | SERVES 1

BANANA ICE-CREAM

INGREDIENTS

4 ripe Bananas

50g Almonds

2 tbsp Maple Syrup

2 tsp Maple Syrup

100ml tinned Coconut Cream

1 tsp Vanilla Extract

METHOD

1. Peel & slice bananas & place them in the freezer for 3 hours.

2. Put almonds in food processor & grind them. Or use 50g of ground almonds. Mix the almonds with two tsp of syrup. And set to one side.

3. In a clean food processor mix the frozen bananas with coconut milk, vanilla & 2 tbsp of syrup.

4. Serve immediately & top with the almond mixture.

MY NOTES

279 KCAL | 12G FAT | 5G PROTEIN | 35G CARBS | SERVES 4

CINNAMON COFFEE CAKE

INGREDIENTS

50g Almond Flour

30g Coconut Flour

30g Desiccated Coconut, unsweetened

4 large Eggs, beaten

50g Coconut Oil, melted

1 small cup of Black Coffee

50ml Almond Milk

1 tsp Baking Powder

1 tsp Bicarbonate of Soda

1 tsp Vanilla Extract

1 tsp Cinnamon

75g Almond Flakes

METHOD

1. Preheat oven to 180c (160 fan), 350f, Gas Mark 4. Grease a square baking dish.

2. In a bowl combine all the dry ingredients.

3. In another bowl beat together the eggs, milk, oil, vanilla extract, coffee, honey. Slowly add dry ingredients & continue to beat until combined. Pour into the greased dish.

4. Cover with tin foil and bake for 15 mins. Remove foil and continue to bake for 5 more mins. Allow to cool before serving.

MY NOTES

322KCAL | 28G FAT | 10G PROTEIN | 8G CARBS | SERVES 8

NUT CHEESE

INGREDIENTS

50g blanched Almonds

75g Walnuts

50g Sunflower Seeds

125ml Water

bunch of fresh Herbs, chopped

a little Nut Butter

METHOD

1. In a bowl grind the nuts & sunflower seed finely, add the water & mix well. Stir in herbs & nut butter.

2. Place the bowl covered with a clean tea towel in a warm place for 12 hours.

3. Once fermented it can be stored in the fridge & served with crudites.

MY NOTES

209 KCAL | 19G FAT | 6G PROTEIN | 5G CARBS | SERVES 6

MINI PROTEIN 'BOUNTY' BARS

MEAL FOR ONE

INGREDIENTS

4 scoops of White Chocolate Protein Powder

100g unsweetened Desiccated Coconut

30g tinned Coconut Milk

100g 70%+ Dark Chocolate

METHOD

1. In a mixing bowl bring together coconut, whey and coconut milk until it forms large firm ball of dough.

2. Place a clean bowl over a saucepan of simmering water. Break chocolate into the bowl. Do not allow water to touch the base of the bowl. Melt the chocolate. Give it a couple of stirs.

3. Use a dessert spoon to size coconut dough, roll in palms of hand into a ball and then shape into a mini bar. Do this 12 times.

4. Using the dessert spoon dip and roll each bar into the melted chocolate and place on a plate. Repeat until 12 bars have been covered.

5. Using a teaspoon, spoon melted chocolate onto top to each bar and smooth. Then move the plate to the fridge to set.

MY NOTES

147 KCAL | 10G FAT | 9G PROTEIN | 3G CARBS | SERVES 12

RUNNERS DATE & APRICOT BARS

MEAL FOR ONE

INGREDIENTS

70g chopped Dates

70g dried ready to eat Apricots

50g Pumpkin Seeds

3 tbsp of Almond Butter

30g Oats

2 scoops of Chocolate Protein Powder

METHOD

1. Place all ingredients except oats in food processor.

2. Pulse & process until forms a sticky dough.

3. Cover a board with greaseproof paper & sprinkle with oats. Place dough on paper, press to 5cm flat and shape into an oblong. Sprinkle top with oats.

4. Chill bar in fridge for at least an hour. Cut into 12 small fingers.

MY NOTES

95KCAL 4G FAT 2G PROTEIN 11G CARBS SERVES 12

PROTEIN CARAMEL COOKIES

INGREDIENTS

50g Almond Flour

2 scoops of Chocolate Whey

50g of mixed Dried Fruit

3 tbsp Coconut Oil, melted

1 Egg

1 tin of Coconut Milk

50g Coconut Sugar

25g of 85% Dark Chocolate

1 tsp Coconut Oil

2 scoops of Chocolate Protein Powder

METHOD

The Base
1. Place the almond flour, chocolate protein powder, dried fruit, the melted coconut oil melted & 1 egg in a food processor pulse ingredients until it forms a sticky dough.
2. Grease a small/mini silicon muffin pan with coconut oil. Use heaped tsp of dough mix to line the base of the mould. Place mould in freezer.

The Middle
3. Heat the coconut milk & coconut sugar in a saucepan at a low rolling boil fo 20-30 mins, stirring regularly, until pan contents have reduced by half & make a thick toffee sauce.
4. Using half the sauce, pour a little into the moulds & return them to the freezer.

The Top
5. Return pan to the heat with half the toffee sauce. Add coconut oil, chocolate stir. Once melted stir in chocolate protein powder. Top up the moulds with this chocolate sauce & return to the freezer.

6. Leave for up to 4 hours. Pop the caramel cookies out of the moulds. Store in the freezer & remove 15 mins before eating.

MY NOTES

104 KCAL | 6G FAT | 6G PROTEIN | 7G CARBS | SERVES 20

CARROT CAKE

INGREDIENTS

2 Carrots, grated
1 Egg
1 Vanilla Pod, seeds scrapped
2 tsp Ground Ginger
½ tsp Nutmeg
100ml Almond MilK
100g Almond Flour
1 tsp Baking Powder
50g Applesauce, unsweet-ened

Icing
splash Almond Milk
5 tbsp Almond Butter

METHOD

1. Preheat oven to 180c (160 fan), 350f, Gas Mark 4. Grease small loaf tin, or use a silicon one.

2. In a bowl mix together the flour, spices & baking powder.

3. In a separate bowl whisk together applesauce, egg, milk, vanilla, carrots. Slowly mix this into the flour mix.

4. Pour cake batter into the loaf tin and bake for 30mins. If the top of the loaf appears to be 'catching' cover with foil.

5. Allow cake to cool a little. Remove from loaf tin.

6. In a small bowl beat almond butter with little almond milk to thin slightly. Glaze the top of the loaf.

MY NOTES

226KCAL | 18G FAT | 9G PROTEIN | 8G CARBS | SERVES 6

FRENCH PATE

INGREDIENTS

500g Pork Fillet, diced

500g Pork Belly, diced

750g Chicken Livers, chopped

4 tbsp Balsamic Vinegar

4 tsp fresh Thyme, chopped

Olive Oil for greasing

12 rashers Streaky Bacon

METHOD

1. In a large bowl mix together all the ingredients, except bacon, cover & place in fridge to marinate for 2 hours.

2. Preheat oven to 180 c (160 fan), 350f, Gas Mark 4.

3. Using a knife stretch the bacon rashers. Grease large loaf tin. Pile in marinated ingredients & cover with bacon.

4. Cover the loaf tin with foil. Place in roasting tin and fill tin with enough boiling water to reach half way up the loaf. Bake for 1 hour 30 mins.

5. Leave to cool in the loaf tin and only turn out when cold. Can be stored covered in fridge.

MY NOTES

172 KCAL | 13G FAT | 14G PROTEIN | 0G CARBS | SERVES 16

38617694R00084

Made in the USA
Charleston, SC
10 February 2015